THE PETERSBURG AND APPOMATTOX CAMPAIGNS

1864–1865

by
John R. Maass

Center of Military History
United States Army
Washington, D.C., 2015

INTRODUCTION

Although over one hundred fifty years have passed since the start of the American Civil War, that titanic conflict continues to matter. The forces unleashed by that war were immensely destructive because of the significant issues involved: the existence of the Union, the end of slavery, and the very future of the nation. The war remains our most contentious, and our bloodiest, with over six hundred thousand killed in the course of the four-year struggle.

Most civil wars do not spring up overnight, and the American Civil War was no exception. The seeds of the conflict were sown in the earliest days of the republic's founding, primarily over the existence of slavery and the slave trade. Although no conflict can begin without the conscious decisions of those engaged in the debates at that moment, in the end, there was simply no way to paper over the division of the country into two camps: one that was dominated by slavery and the other that sought first to limit its spread and then to abolish it. Our nation was indeed "half slave and half free," and that could not stand.

Regardless of the factors tearing the nation asunder, the soldiers on each side of the struggle went to war for personal reasons: looking for adventure, being caught up in the passions and emotions of their peers, believing in the Union, favoring states' rights, or even justifying the simple schoolyard dynamic of being convinced that they were "worth" three of the soldiers on the other side. Nor can we overlook the factor that some went to war to prove their manhood. This has been, and continues to be, a key dynamic in understanding combat and the profession of arms. Soldiers join for many reasons but often stay in the fight because of their comrades and because they do not want to seem like cowards. Sometimes issues of national impact shrink to nothing in the intensely personal world of cannon shell and minié ball.

Whatever the reasons, the struggle was long and costly and only culminated with the conquest of the rebellious Confederacy, the preservation of the Union, and the end of slavery. These campaign pamphlets on the American Civil War, prepared in commemoration of our national sacrifices, seek to remember that war and honor those in the United States Army who died to preserve the Union and free the slaves as well as to tell the story of those American soldiers who fought for the Confederacy despite the inherently flawed nature of their cause. The Civil War was our greatest struggle and continues to deserve our deep study and contemplation.

RICHARD W. STEWART
Chief Historian

The Petersburg and Appomattox Campaigns 1864–1865

Strategic Setting

By mid-June 1864, Lt. Gen. Ulysses S. Grant, commander of all United States armies fighting to defeat the Confederate rebellion, faced a strategic dilemma at his headquarters near Cold Harbor, Virginia. Under his close control, the Union Army of the Potomac led by Maj. Gen. George G. Meade had just battled 66,000 rebels of General Robert E. Lee's formidable Army of Northern Virginia in a bloody, month-long campaign. Beginning on 4 May, when Meade's 100,000 troops had marched south across the Rapidan River west of Fredericksburg, the opposing armies had been in almost constant contact. Grant had sought to bring Lee's army to battle and to destroy it with the Federals' superior numbers, but Lee had deftly thwarted Grant's flanking maneuvers in the battles of the Wilderness (5–6 May), Spotsylvania Court House (8–21 May), and the North Anna River (23–26 May). After each battle, Grant had attempted to outflank Lee's entrenched position by moving to the Union left to prevent the rebels from falling back to strong defenses and to force them to fight in the open. The Confederate commander had successfully parried each of Grant's thrusts and positioned his force between the Union army and Richmond, the Confederate capital.

But Grant was not easily discouraged. Born in Ohio, he had graduated from the United States Military Academy at West Point in 1843, and had served in the Mexican War. After that, his Army career took a downward turn, and he resigned his commission in 1854 amid accusations of chronic drunkenness. Later, several business ventures and attempts at farming ended in failure, and by 1860, he was working at his father's tannery in Galena, Illinois. The outbreak of the Civil War saw Grant back in uniform, first organizing

General Grant
(Library of Congress)

new state units, then as a regimental commander, and he was soon promoted to brigadier general. Grant's fortunes rose rapidly, as he earned a second star and won impressive victories at Fort Donelson and Shiloh in Tennessee, at Vicksburg, Mississippi, and at Chattanooga, Tennessee. President Abraham Lincoln was impressed by Grant's successes and secured his promotion to lieutenant general in March 1864. Now in command of all Federal armies, Grant chose to make his headquarters in the field with Meade's army, which had won few victories against the rebels in the war's Eastern Theater. Grant's presence with the Army of the Potomac was awkward and tended to undermine Meade's authority, but the latter kept his command until the war's end.

On 26 May, Grant had ordered Meade to move the Army of the Potomac southeast across the Pamunkey River for a drive against Richmond, and by 31 May, Federal cavalry had reached the crossroads hamlet of Cold Harbor, nine miles northeast of the Confederate capital. Already entrenched and waiting for the Union troops nearby were Lee's veteran soldiers. After several ineffective Federal attacks on 1 and 2 June, Grant had ordered

Meade to launch a morning assault with all of his troops against the rebels' seven-mile line of earthworks on 3 June. The result had been a disaster for the Northern soldiers. At a cost of roughly 6,000 dead and wounded, the Federals could make no headway and ceased their attacks soon after they were launched. In contrast, Lee's army had lost no more than 1,500 men that day and remained behind strong fieldworks, still blocking Grant's path to Richmond. Nevertheless, Lee had lost over 30,000 troops since the Battle of the Wilderness, and those losses could not be easily replaced.

Grant's predicament was how to annihilate Lee's army and capture Richmond with an army that had suffered about 55,000 casualties since crossing the Rapidan River. In addition to these military considerations, Grant was mindful of certain political factors. His continual hammering of Lee's army generated long Union casualty lists, which in turn demoralized the Northern populace. War-weary critics of Grant's costly operations pointed out that his army was now exactly where Maj. Gen. George B. McClellan had brought the Army of the Potomac during his own campaign against Richmond in 1862—with far fewer casualties. A month's fighting in Virginia under Grant's leadership seemed to have brought the Union no closer to victory, resulting in a disheartened Northern public that might spell political trouble for Lincoln in the upcoming presidential election.

Across the lines, a combination of optimism and realism prevailed among the Confederate soldiers and their leaders. Lee's troops had inflicted massive casualties on the Federal invaders and had prevented them from taking Richmond, while other Confederate forces had simultaneously blocked Union offensives in the Shenandoah Valley and along the James River south of the rebel capital. Most of Lee's soldiers had remained in good spirits and were confident of defeating the Federals. Yet Lee's losses were difficult to replace given the South's worsening manpower shortage. Moreover, his army had lost many experienced officers from wounds, illness, and death since the spring fighting had commenced, including four veteran corps commanders: Lt. Gens. James Longstreet, Richard S. Ewell, and Ambrose Powell Hill, and Maj. Gen. J. E. B. Stuart.

The heavy casualties had revealed that the Army of Northern Virginia's greatest strength lay in its commander. The Virginia-born Lee had enjoyed a stellar military career prior to the Civil War, beginning with his U.S. Military Academy graduation in 1829, where he ranked second in his class. He went on to serve conspicuously as Maj. Gen. Winfield Scott's chief engineer during the Mexican War and as superintendant of West Point from 1852 to 1855. Lincoln's trusted adviser Francis P. Blair Sr. discussed political affairs with Lee and offered him the command of U.S. forces in the early days of the Civil War, but Lee declined, citing his duty to Virginia, which had seceded from the Union. Instead, Lee entered the Confederate army, in which his initial service earned him few laurels. In May 1862, however, Lee assumed command of the Army of Northern Virginia, and began a brilliant career by defeating several larger Union armies, first around Richmond in the Seven Days Battles, followed by victories at Second Bull Run, Fredericksburg, and Chancellorsville. Although the Army of the Potomac had turned back Lee's two invasions of the North at Antietam, Maryland, and Gettysburg, Pennsylvania, he remained a dangerous and resourceful foe in June 1864.

General Lee
(Library of Congress)

Lee did not doubt his troops' ability to fight behind breastworks, but by mid-June, he grimly concluded that "something more is necessary than adhering to lines and defensive positions." Having repulsed the bluecoats once again at Cold Harbor from behind strong defenses, he waited to see what the Federals' next move would be. Lee was anxious about the strength of Union forces, Grant's hammer blows, and their imminent threat to Richmond. "We must destroy this army of Grant's before he gets to James River," Lee observed, for "if he gets there it will become a siege, and then it will be a mere question of time."

Soon after the Federals' failed frontal assaults at Cold Harbor on 3 June, Grant decided to change tactics. Rather than attacking Richmond directly, he opted to disrupt the rebels' logistical network in Virginia in order to force Lee to abandon Richmond's defenses due to a lack of supplies. Grant hoped this would allow Federal

General Sheridan
(Library of Congress)

forces to bring Lee's troops to battle in the open, where superior numbers would give the Northern army a decided advantage. To begin his three-pronged movement to force the rebels to abandon their capital, Grant utilized a powerful cavalry force under the impetuous Maj. Gen. Philip H. Sheridan, "a terror to his foes," as one of his peers described him. On 7 June, Sheridan rode west from Hanover with two divisions to damage the Virginia Central Railroad, Richmond's main supply artery from Charlottesville. Sheridan also planned to link up with a small Union force under Maj. Gen. David Hunter, then at Staunton, but ran into enemy troopers on 11–12 June, at Trevilian Station on the Virginia Central twenty-five miles east of Charlottesville. After a bloody two-day battle with most of Lee's cavalry under Maj. Gen. Wade Hampton, Sheridan had to abandon his Charlottesville raid and return to the Army of the Potomac east of Richmond.

Grant's primary thrust was an effort to deceive Lee by holding him in place north of the James River, while the bulk of the Army of the Potomac crossed the river to Virginia's Southside region, marching quickly on to Petersburg, twenty-four miles south of Richmond. This lightly defended city—the seventh largest in the South—was the major rail hub of the

Southern supply system in Virginia. A branch of the South Side Railroad ran ten miles northeast from Petersburg to City Point on the James River, while the Norfolk and Petersburg Railroad led southeast to the lower Tidewater region. The South Side Railroad also linked Petersburg with Lynchburg, about one hundred miles to the west, as well as with supply sources in Tennessee. The crucial Petersburg and Weldon line (often called the Weldon Railroad) connected Lee's forces with North Carolina, particularly the port of Wilmington, where the road terminated. A single track, the Richmond and Petersburg Railroad, connected the two cities, while the rebel capital also received supplies via the Virginia Central and the Richmond and Danville Railroad. Grant surmised that the capture of Petersburg would cripple the Confederacy's ability to resist Union forces in Virginia, and ultimately lead to Lee's defeat.

Grant's movement against Petersburg, however, would leave Washington, D.C., potentially exposed to Confederate attack, a scenario that had alarmed the Lincoln administration in the past. This decision, a Northern newspaper reporter later wrote, "involved considerations of a wholly different order from those concerned in the repeated turning movements which he [Grant] had made to dislodge Lee" in May and June. Crossing the James River meant the "total abandonment of that system of action which aimed . . . to directly defend the national capital." Lincoln approved Grant's plan, though not without misgivings for the Northern capital's safety.

Grant included a third advance in his May plans, to be conducted by the Federal Army of the James under Maj. Gen. Benjamin F. Butler, a politically appointed general with little military skill or initiative. Several weeks earlier, Butler's 35,000 troops had landed at Bermuda Hundred, a peninsula situated between the James and Appomattox Rivers south of Richmond, where they were easily supplied by Union shipping. He also had troops occupy City Point. Ordered to march on Richmond while the Army of the Potomac faced off against Lee's soldiers in the Wilderness, Butler instead had sent almost 22,000 troops against Petersburg. In a series of engagements with outnumbered rebel defenders under General P. G. T. Beauregard, Butler's force had failed to take the town. He had brought all of his men back to Bermuda Hundred by 22 May and had them dig a north–south defensive line across his entire front, after which he remained inactive. "Butler's position was like a bottle," Grant concluded, and his entrenchments "represented the cork." In short, the hapless Butler could do nothing offensively.

On 9 June, Butler again tried to capture Petersburg, this time with a column of 6,500 men under Maj. Gen. Quincy A. Gillmore, but the troops had little time to prepare for the operation. An assorted force of 1,000 Confederate soldiers, town militia, and civilian volunteers led by Brig. Gen. Henry A. Wise, a former Virginia governor, managed to turn back the bluecoats by the afternoon. The Union attacks were poorly coordinated, and Butler missed an opportunity to capture Petersburg before Confederate authorities could reinforce the city's few defenders. A thoroughly disgusted Butler relieved Gillmore of his command once his dispirited men had returned to Union lines.

CROSSING THE JAMES RIVER

Attempting to avoid detection, the Army of the Potomac withdrew from its long line of fieldworks at Cold Harbor and moved south toward the James River over several dusty roads beginning on 12 June. Maj. Gen. William F. "Baldy" Smith's XVIII Corps, part of Butler's army but then serving with Meade, marched to White House on the Pamunkey River—where the men destroyed the large Union supply depot and rail line before boarding transport ships for a water passage to Bermuda Hundred—to reunite with the Army of the James. On the Union left, the V Corps under Maj. Gen. Gouverneur K. Warren marched south behind a cavalry screen, crossed the Chickahominy River, and turned west to make a feint toward Richmond—and to block rebel attempts to strike the Federals en route to the James River (*Map 1*).

After nightfall on the twelfth, Maj. Gen. Horatio G. Wright's VI Corps and Maj. Gen. Winfield S. Hancock's II Corps withdrew to a shorter line of fieldworks recently erected in Meade's rear before their march south. Maj. Gen. Ambrose E. Burnside took his IX Corps on a longer route to the James to avoid congestion on the roads, followed by a cavalry rear guard. By 14 June, all of the Union corps—numbering about 115,000 men—had reached the James River. Hancock's men crossed by boat at Wilcox's Landing on the river, as did the V Corps. Three miles downstream, the rest of the army—including its wagons and artillery—began crossing on 15 June, on a 2,100-foot pontoon bridge constructed at Wyanoke Neck the previous day by the army's engineers. "Our movement from Cold Harbor to the James River has been made

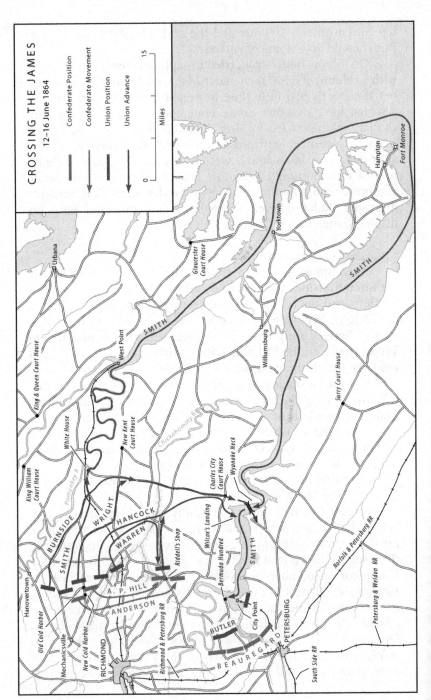

CROSSING THE JAMES
12–16 June 1864

Confederate Position
Confederate Movement
Union Position
Union Advance

0 — 15 Miles

Urbana

Gloucester Court House

Hampton

Fort Monroe

Yorktown

SMITH

SMITH

King & Queen Court House

West Point

SMITH

Williamsburg

York R.

Surry Court House

King William Court House

White House

New Kent Court House

Chickahominy R.

Charles City Court House

Wyanoke Neck

James R.

Pamunkey R.

BURNSIDE

SMITH

WRIGHT

HANCOCK

WARREN

Riddell's Shop

Wilcox's Landing

Bermuda Hundred

SMITH

Norfolk & Petersburg RR

Hanovertown

Old Cold Harbor

Mechanicsville

New Cold Harbor

A. P. HILL

ANDERSON

RICHMOND

Richmond & Petersburg RR

BUTLER

City Point

PETERSBURG

BEAUREGARD

South Side RR

Petersburg & Weldon RR

MAP 1

with great celerity," Grant proudly reported. All but a few Federal units had reached the south bank of the James by midnight of 16 June, including Smith's XVIII Corps, which had previously landed at Bermuda Hundred.

General Lee learned at dawn on 13 June that the Federals at Cold Harbor had left his immediate front but he was uncertain where the bluecoats had gone. He began shifting his men south of the Chickahominy River to cover Richmond's southeast approaches against the prospect of another of Grant's flanking maneuvers. After an inconclusive engagement with mounted Union covering forces near Riddell's Shop later that day, he surmised that Grant was headed for the James River but could not be sure. Meanwhile other Union operations distracted the Confederate commander. Both Lee and the Confederate War Department had been receiving urgent requests from Beauregard at Petersburg for more troops, along with a warning that he had too few men to contain Butler within Bermuda Hundred. Moreover, after the Battle of Cold Harbor, Lee had detached from his army Maj. Gen. John C. Breckinridge's division and Maj. Gen. Jubal A. Early's Second Corps to counter Hunter's threatening operations in the Shenandoah Valley. Consequently, the Confederates now confronted Grant's armies with greatly reduced numbers.

An Opportunity Lost

The well-executed maneuver to bring the Army of the Potomac across the James River while keeping Lee unsure of his intentions gave Grant the initiative, but Union forces still had to exploit the enemy's confusion. Grant envisioned a quick strike to seize Petersburg before the rebels could react and shift troops south from Richmond. After conferring with Butler at Bermuda Hundred on 14 June, Grant ordered him to have General Smith cross the Appomattox River and move south on 15 June with the XVIII Corps—reinforced by Federal cavalry and a division of U.S. Colored Troops (USCT)—to attack Petersburg. Hancock's II Corps, which had already crossed the James River, would support Smith's assault. Early on the fifteenth, Smith advanced toward Petersburg with 15,000 men and began his attack by 0700 on the city's poorly prepared eastern fortifications. Called the Dimmock Line, the ten-mile defensive system was manned by just 4,000 rebels (*Map 2*).

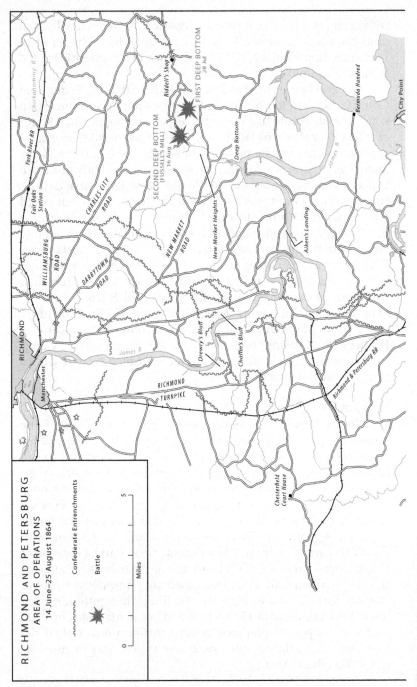

RICHMOND AND PETERSBURG
AREA OF OPERATIONS
14 June–25 August 1864

Confederate Entrenchments

Battle

0   5
Miles

MAP 2

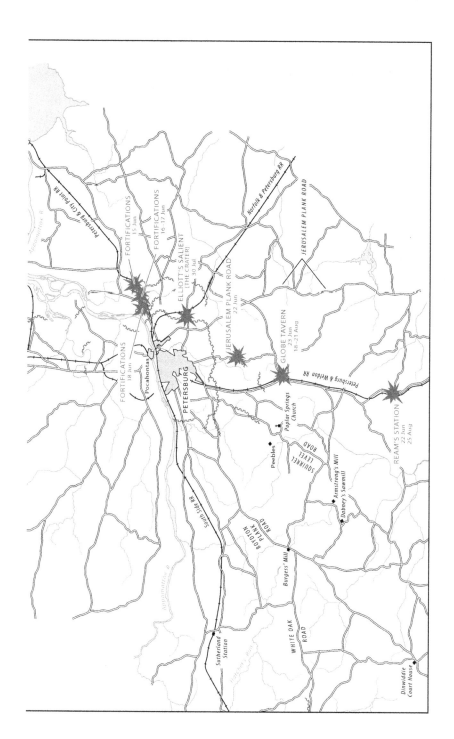

The operation soon succumbed to a series of delays, as Smith, hesitant about charging rebel earthworks, made a lengthy reconnaissance of the enemy's lines. Smith's concern proved unfounded, for when he finally launched his assault at 1900, his men overran much of the Confederate defenses. U.S. Colored Troops under Brig. Gen. Edward W. Hinks captured several rebel batteries that evening, and one of their white officers wrote that the black soldiers "behaved in such a manner as to give me great satisfaction and the fullest confidence in the fighting qualities of colored troops." Petersburg was now open to capture and "at the mercy of the Federal commander," wrote Beauregard, whose troops retreated to a position behind Harrison's Creek, just east of the city. Smith, however, halted on the outskirts, wary of rumored rebel reinforcements nearby. Due to uncertainty over his orders and costly delays in resupplying his men, Hancock was late in coming to Smith's support and did not press the latter for a renewed advance.

In the meantime, Beauregard's urgent pleas for support finally prompted Lee to send Maj. Gen. Robert F. Hoke's division to Petersburg on 15 June. Beauregard also stripped the Confederate defenses at Bermuda Hundred of troops from Maj. Gen. Bushrod R. Johnson's division, and brought them south to oppose Smith's advance. By now Lee recognized the imminent threat to the city and began to shift even more troops there. By the morning of 16 June, Beauregard's defenders numbered about 14,000 men behind the earthworks east of the city, facing the Union II and XVIII Corps, as well as Burnside's newly arrived IX Corps. Meade and Grant were both on the scene, but the Federals did not manage to launch an attack until late that afternoon without substantial success. "In all this we lost very heavily," Grant noted. Repeated attacks by Union forces on 17 June—augmented by Warren's V Corps—pushed back Beauregard's defensive lines, but Lee reinforced him, and again the Federals suffered heavy casualties.

On the next day, a frustrated Meade ordered a general assault on the city from the Appomattox River to the Norfolk and Petersburg Railroad. "If we can engage [the enemy] before they are fortified we ought to whip them," he advised the II Corps commander, but by dusk, the uncoordinated assaults made by the exhausted Union soldiers had failed. Lee had arrived earlier that day to assume direction of the battle, along with substantial infantry reinforcements, including A. P. Hill's Third Corps and two divisions of Lt. Gen. Richard H. Anderson's First Corps.

For the Federals, the opportunity to seize Petersburg and to deal a crippling blow to the enemy's logistical center was lost along with over 10,000 casualties since 15 June. General Smith should have advanced into the city on the night of the fifteenth, but he had allowed darkness and limited rebel opposition to stall his attack. "I believed then," Grant later recalled, "and still believe, that Petersburg could have been easily captured at that time." Instead, Meade ordered his Federals to dig earthworks after the failed 18 June attacks, beginning a grinding campaign that ultimately lasted ten months. The Confederates lost 4,000 men in successfully defending Petersburg, yet Lee had larger concerns. He had failed to strike a blow against the Federals on their march to the James, and now his army faced the prospect of defending Petersburg and Richmond against a superior foe. Once again the rebels had lost the initiative to Grant.

Maneuvering Around Petersburg, 22 June–29 July

Despite having squandered an opportunity to capture Petersburg, Grant had no intention of settling into a protracted siege of the city: "I have determined to try to envelope Petersburg," Grant wrote to Butler. The Union II Corps—now temporarily led by Maj. Gen. David B. Birney in place of General Hancock, whose Gettysburg wound had reopened—and Wright's VI Corps marched south on 22 June behind the Federal lines to Meade's left flank along the Jerusalem Plank Road, which ran south from the city. Grant intended for the II Corps to capture and destroy the Weldon Railroad, about two miles west of the Jerusalem Plank Road. Meanwhile, Wright's men would swing around to Petersburg's northwest side to damage the South Side Railroad and position its left flank on the Appomattox River. The V, IX, and XVIII Corps remained in their trenches east of the city, as the army was "exhausted with forty-nine days of continued marching and fighting," reported General Meade, "and absolutely requires rest to prevent its morale being impaired."

On the morning of 22 June, the II and VI Corps were aligned parallel to the Jerusalem Plank Road, with Birney's men north of Wright's corps. The II Corps wheeled northwest against the enemy works, with its right flank in contact with the entrenched V Corps to the east. As part of their great turning movement to reach the

Appomattox River, Wright's troops first proceeded directly west toward the Weldon Railroad, beginning in the II Corps' left rear, but as Birney moved forward at 1400, the thickly wooded terrain caused his troops to lose contact with the VI Corps. As both corps advanced, a dangerous gap soon opened between them.

Given the vital importance of maintaining the supply lines to Lee's army, rebel troops from Hill's Third Corps on the western flank reacted quickly to the Federal miscue. Recognizing the widening gap between the II and VI Corps as they advanced, about midafternoon of 22 June, Confederates under Brig. Gen. William Mahone (temporarily commanding Anderson's division of Hill's Third Corps) left their Petersburg trenches, pushed through the gap by way of a large concealed ravine, and attacked Birney's left and rear. Mahone's charging rebels panicked much of Birney's command, which, as one Federal wrote, "was thrown into confusion by a sharp attack of the enemy in great force." Grant later described the II Corps' ensuing retreat as a "stampede." Mahone's soldiers rounded up about 1,700 Union prisoners in the dense thickets before their attack stalled that evening in front of makeshift Union breastworks. Hill also ordered Maj. Gen. Cadmus M. Wilcox's division to attack in support of Mahone, but Wilcox could not bring his brigades into action due to the dense undergrowth that obstructed his men. That night, Hill withdrew his victorious troops to the Petersburg lines, with four captured Union cannons in tow.

On the following day, part of Wright's VI Corps and a small force of Union cavalry reached the Weldon Railroad west of Globe Tavern, where they destroyed a one-quarter-mile section of the tracks. Hill sent General Wilcox's division south along the railroad to counter the Federal advance. Late that afternoon, the Confederates struck the VI Corps' pickets on the left flank, capturing 400 Federals and pushing the rest back. The rebel assault thoroughly confused Wright about the enemy's intent and location, and led him to withdraw his bluecoats to their entrenchments by midnight, despite Meade's injunction to "take the initiative and attack the enemy." Hill likewise recalled his Southern troops to the Petersburg lines that night. Although Meade's soldiers had failed to seize the vital Weldon Railroad, the Army of the Potomac did extend its lines to the west, and further threatened Lee's supply lines.

Meanwhile, an Army of the Potomac cavalry division led by Brig. Gen. James H. Wilson, augmented by Brig. Gen. August V. Kautz's mounted division from Butler's army, left Petersburg on 22 June to destroy rail lines west and southwest of the city. If successful, the raid would leave Lee with only the Virginia Central Railroad to supply his army. Wilson's 5,000 mounted men hit the Weldon line at Ream's Station south of Petersburg and then quickly moved west along the South Side Railroad, following it to Burkeville and destroying sections of track as they proceeded. On 25 June, Kautz's men tried to burn the Richmond and Danville Railroad bridge over the Staunton River forty miles southwest of Burkeville, but local defense forces drove them off. Pressed in the rear by rebel cavalry under Maj. Gen. William H. F. "Rooney" Lee and one hundred miles from his base near Petersburg, Wilson elected to return east to Union lines. On 28 June, his troopers ran into Confederate cavalry under General Hampton on the Weldon Railroad at Stony Creek Station, about twenty-five miles south of Petersburg. Forced northward to Ream's Station and then cut off by Mahone's rebel infantry,

Kautz's Cavalry coming back to camp in General Butler's lines after their raid, *by William Waud*
(Library of Congress)

Wilson and Kautz separated there on 29 June and made their way back to Union lines while pursued by swarming Southern horsemen. Back in camp by 1 July, Wilson's force had destroyed sixty miles of railroad track, but at a cost of almost 1,500 casualties during the 300-mile expedition.

In early July, General Grant took stock of the recent operations of Birney and Wright along the Jerusalem Plank Road—coupled with the Wilson-Kautz cavalry raid— and decided that they marked a crucial turning point in the campaign. With Butler's troops "bottled up" at Bermuda Hundred north of the James River and Meade's Army of the Potomac unable to make any headway against Lee's defenses south of the river, Grant concluded that the siege of Petersburg had begun.

First Battle of Deep Bottom, 27–28 July

Despite the seemingly static nature of siege warfare, Union forces around Richmond and Petersburg did not abandon offensive operations. The Federals began to prepare for an assault against Lee's lines east of the city, primarily in front of the Union center held by Burnside's IX Corps. With Hancock back in command, the II Corps was dug in on Burnside's right flank up to the Appomattox River, and Warren's V Corps held the Union left,

Union pontoon bridge on the James River at Deep Bottom
(Library of Congress)

south to the Jerusalem Plank Road; both were expected to support the main assault by Burnside.

In order to draw Confederate troops away from the section of Petersburg defenses that Burnside planned to attack, Grant ordered the II Corps and two divisions of cavalry under Sheridan to cross the James River at Deep Bottom to join Butler's Army of the James facing Richmond. Hancock's men would move toward the city, while Sheridan dashed into the enemy capital, or failing that, strike the enemy's lines of communications northwest of Richmond. "The plan . . . was to let the cavalry cut loose," Grant wrote, "and destroy as much as they could of the Virginia Central Railroad." In the predawn darkness of 27 July, Hancock and Sheridan crossed the James via a pontoon bridge to Deep Bottom on the river's north bank.

Opposing Hancock and Sheridan's advance on Richmond was Anderson's First Corps, whose troops blocked the Union advance along New Market Heights and Bailey's Creek. Lee hurried reinforcements to Anderson from Petersburg, leaving only 18,000 troops to defend the city. On 28 July, Sheridan fought off a determined Confederate attack east of Hancock's foot soldiers near Riddell's Shop, but could not get around the enemy's left to execute his planned raid. "The fighting lasted for several hours, resulting in considerable loss to both sides," noted Grant, who did not want Hancock "to assault intrenched lines." Hancock and Sheridan brought their troops back to the Petersburg front on 29 July, without endangering Richmond, but having forced Lee to reduce his forces south of the James.

THE CRATER

While Hancock and Sheridan moved against Richmond and the rail lines north of the James River, Meade and his subordinates prepared a major assault against Lee's weakened defenses at Petersburg. In the IX Corps' sector, the 48th Pennsylvania Infantry was positioned only 400 feet from the Confederate stronghold called Elliott's (or Pegram's) Salient. Recruited from a mining region around Scranton in 1861, the regiment's ranks were filled with coal miners, and its commander, Lt. Col. Henry C. Pleasants, had been a professional mining and railroad engineer before the war. Pleasants presented a plan to dig a mine under the enemy's works opposite the 48th Pennsylvania's position and to ignite a huge charge of powder at the end of the tunnel. Once exploded, Pleasants suggested, Union troops would rush forward to breach the rebel lines, overwhelming the startled defenders. Burnside favored the idea, but Meade and his staff opposed it as impractical. Grant, however, was intrigued and ordered the plan to proceed.

The Pennsylvanians began working on 25 June. Within four weeks, they had dug a 5-foot-high tunnel that stretched for 511 feet and ran 20 feet beneath the Confederate trenches manned by Brig. Gen. Stephen Elliott Jr.'s South Carolina brigade, which was dug in about one-quarter-mile east of the Jerusalem Plank Road. Union soldiers filled the end of the shaft with four tons of powder, packed it with sandbags to force the explosion upward, and were ready to detonate the charge on 28 July. Although Brig. Gen. Edward Porter Alexander, the First Corps' chief of artillery, suspected that the Federals were digging a mine and informed General Lee of his hunch, the Confederates failed to locate Pleasants' tunnel.

With the approval of Grant and Meade, General Burnside planned to launch his assault on Elliott's Salient with about 15,000 IX Corps men, many of whom had little combat experience. Burnside initially intended to place Brig. Gen. Edward Ferrero's large division of USCTs at the point of attack, followed by the IX Corps' three all-white divisions, and he began working out the details with his subordinates accordingly. General Meade, however, objected to deploying the black troops in front because they were untested, fearing that if the Union attack failed, the army's leaders would be blamed for sacrificing the black division. Supported by Grant, he ordered Burnside to use one of his white divisions to lead the charge, which gave the IX Corps commander only twelve hours to alter his arrangements. Meade also ordered that after breaching the enemy's lines, Burnside's troops were to "push at once for the crest of Cemetery Hill," the high ground in the rebels' rear that also dominated the city, rather than expand the breach to the right and left. Supporting the IX Corps' attack were several divisions from the II, V, and XVIII Corps (now commanded by Maj. Gen. Edward O. C. Ord, after Baldy Smith's removal on 19 July), and one division from the X Corps, Army of the James.

After some delay caused by faulty fuses, about 0445 on 30 July, the mine exploded, blowing a huge gap in the Confederate line and killing or wounding hundreds of rebels. "The earth seemed to tremble and the next instant there was a report that seemed to deafen all nature," wrote a Confederate officer. A nearby Union soldier noted that the blast was "a magnificent spectacle," in which a "mass of earth went up into the air, carrying with it men, guns, carriages, and timbers, and spread out like an immense cloud." Burnside's men were also stunned by the explosion, and many were unprepared for the dawn assault once the dust and debris had begun to settle. "The whole scene of the explosion struck every one dumb with astonishment," a Federal officer wrote. "The Crater," as the excavation was later dubbed, measured about 25 feet deep, 150 feet wide, and 200 feet long.

Explosion of the Mine on 30 July 1864 from a sketch by Alfred R. Waud
(Library of Congress)

Ten minutes after the blast, the IX Corps troops advanced into and around the crater, but the assault was disjointed and poorly led. It was, as a Union officer wrote, a "wretched disaster." Many of the units became intermingled as curious soldiers paused to look into the huge hole. The incompetence and drunkenness of the lead division commander, Brig. Gen. James H. Ledlie, who had made no effort to prepare his troops for the attack, only added to the chaos. Confused officers and men charged into the breach but hesitated to press on to the high ground beyond the crater as planned. Instead, most of the attackers loitered in and around the crater, rather than move forward as ordered. "Had they done this, I have every reason to believe that Petersburg would have fallen," Grant later wrote. Meade repeatedly ordered Burnside to push the attack, but no amount of prodding could restart the disorientated

Federals, whose division commanders had remained far to the rear instead of supervising the assault.

Rebel batteries poured a deadly fire into the Federals at the crater where Burnside's brigades piled on each other. Enemy mortar shells lobbed into the crater took a lethal toll on the closely packed bluecoats seeking shelter there. General Lee ordered Mahone to counterattack with his division from the Confederate right. Two of Mahone's brigades launched a powerful bayonet charge against Union troops in the breach about 1000. The rebels halted the IX Corps' slow progress and recovered the Confederate trench lines around the crater in bitter hand-to-hand fighting. Many Southern soldiers offered no quarter to Ferrero's black troops trapped in the crater. At 0945, Meade called off the attack, and all Federal units had withdrawn to their own lines by about 1400, having suffered some 3,800 casualties. "It was the saddest affair I have witnessed in this war," Grant wrote. Initially made the scapegoat for the failed attack, Burnside went on leave in mid-August and was never recalled to active military service. Command of the IX Corps devolved on Maj. Gen. John G. Parke, the corps' chief of staff.

FIGHTING ON THE FLANKS, AUGUST 1864

In mid-August, Grant opened a new offensive at Petersburg. The previous month, Lee had detached Early's Second Corps and Breckinridge's division from his army and had sent them to defend the Shenandoah Valley and threaten Washington, D.C. These operations had compelled Grant to hurry General Wright and two divisions of his VI Corps to defend the U.S. capital. Lee also sent additional reinforcements under General Anderson to Early on 6 August, including Maj. Gen. Joseph B. Kershaw's First Corps division, an artillery battalion, and Maj. Gen. Fitzhugh Lee's cavalry division. With Lee's forces thereby reduced, Grant decided to increase pressure on Richmond while Meade's troops moved around the Union left, in another attempt to cut the Weldon Railroad south of Petersburg. "My main object," Grant explained, "is to call troops from Early and from the defenses of Petersburg."

On the night of 13–14 August, Hancock's II Corps returned to Deep Bottom to threaten Richmond with 28,000 men, supported by General Birney's X Corps and Brig. Gen. David M. Gregg's cavalry division. Grant believed that Lee had sent three divisions from Richmond to reinforce Early in the Shenandoah Valley, but in fact only Kershaw's division had left the capital's defenses;

26

consequently, the rebel forces southeast of Richmond were far stronger than Grant and Hancock assumed. On 16 August, the initial Union attacks on the Confederate left along the Darbytown Road near Fussell's Mill shoved back the defenders, opening a gap in the Southern line. But rebel troops of Maj. Gen. Charles W. Field's First Corps division counterattacked and regained their fieldworks several hours later. On the extreme Union right, Confederate horsemen under Rooney Lee blocked Gregg's Federal cavalry from dashing into Richmond. Facing 20,000 Confederates, Hancock withdrew his forces to the Petersburg lines south of the James River on 20 August, having lost almost 3,000 men. Many II Corps officers conceded that their weary troops were "without any spirit" due to the cumulative effects of hard campaigning since May and the extreme summer heat. In the end, neither side had gained an advantage from the Second Battle of Deep Bottom. While Hancock's advance on Richmond was thwarted by Confederate forces, Lee likewise was prevented from sending more reinforcements to the Valley, and he had to weaken the defenses of Petersburg to protect the Confederate capital.

While Hancock advanced on Richmond, Federal troops near Petersburg began another move against the Weldon Railroad. On 18 August, General Warren marched west with his V Corps to Globe Tavern, a prominent two-story brick building two miles south of Petersburg and just east of the Weldon Railroad, which was now in Union hands. Although General Hill's rebel troops launched several powerful attacks through 21 August against Warren's entrenched position north of Globe Tavern—including one on the nineteenth in which almost 3,000 panicked Federals of Brig. Gen. Samuel W. Crawford's division were captured— Hill could not drive off Warren's men who were bolstered by IX Corps reinforcements. To consolidate his hold on the railroad, Warren extended his lines eastward to the existing Union trenches. The loss of the Weldon Railroad at Globe Tavern forced the Confederates to haul supplies by wagon on a circuitous, twenty-four-mile route from Stony Creek Station northward to Petersburg via Dinwiddie Court House.

Grant hoped to capitalize on the V Corps' success by destroying more of the Weldon Railroad. On 24 August, 6,000 men of Hancock's II Corps, back from Deep Bottom with no rest, marched several miles south of Globe Tavern to Ream's Station. Shielded by Gregg's 2,000 cavalrymen, Hancock's column began tearing up track. Learning of the Federals' railroad-wrecking operation near Ream's Station, Lee ordered Hill to attack the unsuspecting bluecoats and prevent further disruption of the rail line. Hill maneuvered around the Union V Corps' position at Globe Tavern, and on the afternoon of 25 August, launched several vigorous attacks against Hancock's position at Ream's Station, which the Federals managed to repulse.

Despite taking heavy casualties, the Confederates were persistent. About 1730, the divisions of Maj. Gen. Henry Heth and Wilcox (under Heth's overall command because General Hill's illness) charged from the west and overran the weak Union defenses along the railroad. The rebels "came at the double-quick, with flashing bayonets, and ringing out their familiar yell," wrote one Federal soldier. Meanwhile, Southern cavalry under General Hampton attacked the II Corps from the south. Hit from two sides and blasted by artillery, many of Hancock's troops fled the field. The Confederates captured about 2,100 demoralized Federals and nine guns. With the timely support of IX Corps reinforcements, Hancock withdrew the beaten remnants of his command to Union lines near the Jerusalem Plank Road, and much to the bluecoats' relief, the victorious Confederates did not pursue them.

After Hancock's defeat at Ream's Station, Grant worked to improve the Union Army's defenses around Petersburg. He had a strong secondary line of earthworks constructed behind the front lines, complete with an extensive network of trenches, artillery emplacements, and forts. The first and second lines stretched for a total of ten miles around Petersburg. Grant also strengthened his headquarters and the massive Union supply depot at City Point. The Northern logistical complex also boasted several hospitals that accommodated up to 10,000 patients, along with over a mile of wharfs, numerous warehouses, and a vast rail yard. As of September, a military railroad ran from the City Point docks to Warren's V Corps posted around Globe Tavern, a fourteen-mile route that carried eighteen trains per day. On a typical day during the siege, the Union Army's logistical apparatus at City Point provided the troops with 100,000 bread rations per day and the animals with 12,000 tons of hay while storing an ample supply of food. A mid-September Confederate cavalry raid led by General Hampton, which netted about 2,500 head of cattle from behind Union lines six miles east of City Point, and a well-founded fear of rebel sabotage, led Union authorities to further strengthen the sprawling depot.

While Union forces improved their defenses, Lee commanded his troops to expand Confederate earthworks to the southwest to protect the South Side Railroad and the Boydton Plank Road, crucial branches of his supply network. Rebels north of the James River also improved their positions—often with slave labor—to defend Richmond, although Lee lacked the soldiers to adequately guard all sections of the Confederate lines. "Without some increase in strength," Lee had written in late August, "I cannot see how we can escape the natural military consequences of the enemy's numerical superiority." Reinforcements for Lee's army would be especially crucial because Lincoln had called for another 500,000 volunteers on 18 July 1864.

AUTUMN OPERATIONS

Lee's decision to extend the rebel works was a prudent one in that Union forces launched a new series of offensives in late September. Grant again sought to pressure Lee by advancing simultaneously north and south of the James River, using both the Army of the Potomac and the Army of the James to prevent the Confederate commander from shifting troops to meet Federal

View of the U.S. Military Railroad in front of Petersburg, *by William Waud* (Library of Congress)

attacks. Moreover, Early's force in the Shenandoah Valley suffered a significant defeat at Winchester on 19 September. The reverse came at the hands of General Sheridan. In August, Grant had sent Sheridan northward to lead the Union forces sent to protect Washington. Early's defeat thus complicated Lee's plans to thwart Grant's ongoing efforts to crush the Army of Northern Virginia (*See Map 3*).

On the night of 28–29 September, Butler sent an assault force across the James River from Bermuda Hundred to Deep Bottom via a pontoon bridge. The force consisted of Birney's X Corps, a division of U.S. Colored Troops from Ord's XVIII Corps, and Kautz's cavalry division. The units moved north to attack strong Confederate positions on New Market Heights. "Under a terrific fire of musketry," the Union attackers, spearheaded by a small brigade of black troops, captured the enemy's works on the second attempt, after the 2,000 Confederate defenders under Brig. Gen. John Gregg had withdrawn eastward in the face of superior numbers. "It was a deadly hailstorm of bullets sweeping men down as hail-stones sweep the leaves from trees," wrote Sgt. Maj. Christian Fleetwood of the 4th USCT, "It was sheer madness." For heroism in the Battle of New Market Heights, twelve USCT soldiers received the Medal of Honor, the first black soldiers to be awarded a United States military decoration.

Meanwhile, the rest of Ord's XVIII Corps crossed the James River on a pontoon bridge at Aiken's Landing, a short distance upstream from Deep Bottom, and began to advance northward to the left of the X Corps. By 0700, Ord's men had attacked and captured the rebel works at Fort Harrison, part of the outer line of Richmond's defenses, suffering significant casualties in the process. At the same time, Birney's troops moved northwest from New Market Heights and assaulted the Confederate trenches north of Fort Harrison. The X Corps units were eventually repulsed at Forts Gilmer and Gregg with heavy losses, especially among the USCTs, some of whom the rebels killed after they had surrendered. General Ord was severely wounded during the fighting around Fort Harrison and remained out of action for over two months.

Just as Grant had intended, Lee had to shift forces from Petersburg's defenses to counter Butler's operations against Richmond north of the James River. The Confederate commander transferred the divisions of Hoke and Field to Chaffin's farm, opposite Fort Harrison, which the rebels intended to recapture. On

30 September, the Confederates attacked the fort with 9,000 men as Lee watched nearby, but they could not dislodge the Federals from their stronghold, losing 1,200 men in "a furious storm of bullets" from the Union defenses.

While Butler's divisions repulsed the enemy assault at Fort Harrison, Meade initiated his operations south of Petersburg early on 30 September. Warren's V Corps marched west from near Globe Tavern, supported by two divisions of Parke's IX Corps and Gregg's cavalry division—a total of 20,000 men. His objective was to turn the Confederate right flank just west of Poplar Springs Church and gain the vital Boydton Plank Road, from which the Union columns could then strike the South Side Railroad. Warren's men captured part of the weakly held rebel lines along the Squirrel Level Road near Peeble's farm in a "magnificent charge," then paused to regroup, as Parke advanced the IX Corps cautiously on Warren's left.

Confederate General Hill, in command of Petersburg's defenses while Lee was north of the James River, reacted quickly to the V Corps' success. From the rebel works defending the road, he sent troops under Generals Heth and Wilcox to contest the

Attempt of the rebels to recapture Fort Harrison, *by William Waud*
(Library of Congress)

31

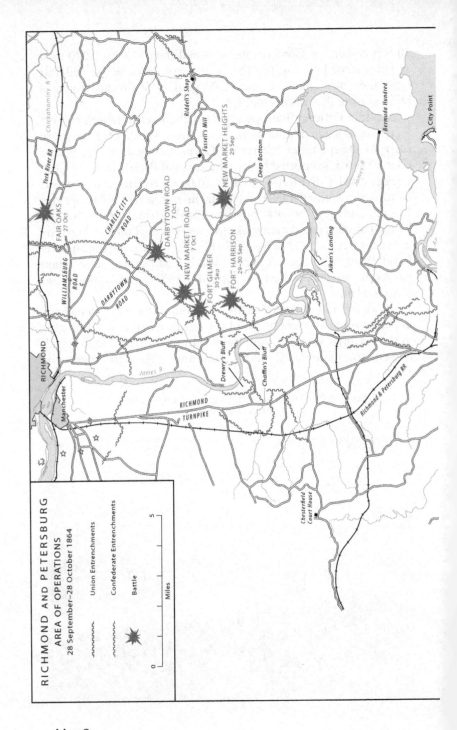

RICHMOND AND PETERSBURG
AREA OF OPERATIONS
28 September–28 October 1864

Union Entrenchments

Confederate Entrenchments

Battle

Miles
0 — 5

MAP 3

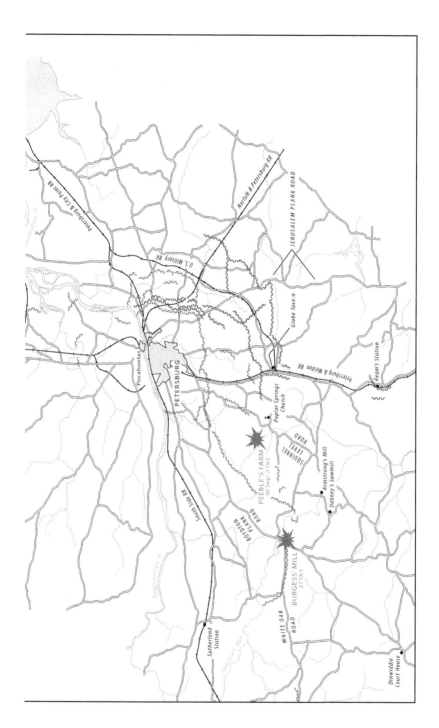

Appomattox R.

Petersburg & City Point RR

Norfolk & Petersburg RR

JERUSALEM PLANK ROAD

U.S. Military RR

Globe Tavern

Pocahontas

Petersburg & Weldon RR

Ream's Station

PETERSBURG

Poplar Springs Church

South Side RR

PEEBLE'S FARM
30 Sep-2 Oct

SQUIRREL LEVEL ROAD

Armstrong's Mill

Dabney's Sawmill

BOYDTON PLANK ROAD

Appomattox R.

BURGESS' MILL
27 Oct

Sutherland Station

Hatcher's Run

WHITE OAK ROAD

Dinwiddie Court House

Union advance. Late on 30 September, Heth's men routed Brig. Gen. Robert B. Potter's IX Corps division and took 1,300 prisoners on the Jones farm near the Boydton Plank Road. At the Pegram farm, Potter rallied most of his panicked troops, formed a line, and advanced his field artillery, which stopped the oncoming rebels. The next day, Warren repulsed another attack by Hill's men at Peeble's farm, and on 2 October, he had part of his troops advance one mile toward the road. Here they entrenched as far west as Pegram's farm, joining their new fieldworks to the existing defensive lines at the Globe Tavern to the east. The Confederate fortifications opposite them were "very formidable," and it "was not deemed advisable to attack," wrote a Northern reporter. Warren had failed to reach his objective, the Boydton Plank Road, but the extension of the Federal siege lines—at the cost of 3,000 men—further stretched Lee's already thin ranks.

While General Hill directed the Confederate operations to counter Warren's attempt to take the Boydton Plank Road, Lee looked for an opportunity to strike at Butler's positions north of the James, particularly at Fort Harrison, which the rebels had been unable to retake on 30 September. Lee planned an attack on the far right flank of the Union lines, to be made by the divisions of Hoke and Field on 7 October. The Confederate foot soldiers routed the Federal cavalry on the Darbytown Road and captured eight cannons, but the Union X Corps repulsed a subsequent assault launched by Field's troops on the New Market Road to the

The Battle of Darbytown Road, *by William Waud*
(Library of Congress)

south. Frustrated that Hoke had failed to properly support Fields' assault, Lee called off further attacks and withdrew his soldiers into Richmond's defensive works, having suffered about 1,300 casualties. The Battle of the Darbytown and New Market Roads proved to be Lee's last offensive effort against the Federals north of the James River. The fighting also cost Lee yet another excellent combat commander, General Gregg, killed while leading the Texas brigade.

Twelve days later, on 19 October, Sheridan won a dramatic victory over Early at Cedar Creek. Sheridan's success in the Shenandoah Valley encouraged the Union. At Meade's suggestion, Grant once again planned to pressure Lee's lines on both sides of the James with simultaneous operations in late October. Butler's troops would move toward Richmond north of the river to distract Lee, while part of Meade's forces marched west to strike the Boydton Plank Road and South Side Railroad beyond the rebels' right flank at Petersburg. Grant did not want Butler to make a full-scale assault on Richmond's extensive fortifications, but rather to demonstrate against the rebels and, if possible, turn their left flank. Grant thus expected Butler's offensive to hold rebel troops north of the river while Union troops moved west of Petersburg.

On a rainy 27 October, Butler sent the X Corps down the Darbytown and Charles City roads toward Richmond. The corps was now under Brig. Gen. Alfred H. Terry, who replaced Birney after the latter had died of malaria earlier that month. Butler also ordered the XVIII Corps, led by his former chief engineer, Brig. Gen. Godfrey Weitzel, north to Fair Oaks on the Williamsburg Road, the site of a battle during the 1862 Peninsula Campaign. The Confederate defenders north of the James were commanded by Lt. Gen. James Longstreet, an experienced corps commander now back with Lee's army after a long recuperation from a serious wound suffered at the Battle of the Wilderness. Longstreet moved most of his men to counter Weitzel's advance after Terry's troops had merely demonstrated along the Darbytown Road. Near Fair Oaks, Weitzel attacked with only two of his seven brigades and was repulsed by Field's rebel division with the "terrific fire of a solid line of infantry," wrote Longstreet. By the end of the fighting, Field's victorious men rounded up 600 Federal prisoners.

The Union high command's objectives for the upcoming Petersburg operation were more ambitious than Butler's had been.

Once again, the main target was the Boydton Plank Road, as Grant continued to direct Union operations against Lee's logistical network. On the morning of 27 October, General Hancock pulled two of his II Corps divisions out of the Federal trench lines east of Petersburg to advance against the rebel right flank on the Boydton Plank Road. The II Corps was aided by the V and IX Corps' diversionary attacks on the rebel lines to the north, while Gregg's Union cavalrymen protected the II Corps' left—or southern—flank and rear as the foot soldiers moved toward Burgess' Mill on Hatcher's Run, the western end of the Confederate line. Hancock's assault force numbered over 30,000 troops.

On the Union right, Parke's IX Corps troops encountered strong enemy fieldworks, and by 0900 his attempt to break through Lee's lines had failed. On the Federal left, however, Hancock's II Corps column had crossed Hatcher's Run by 1200 and reached the Boydton Plank Road near Burgess' Mill, at the intersection with White Oak Road. At this crossroads, Hancock halted his weary troops. Meade realized that a mile of dense woodland now separated the II Corps and Warren's V Corps in the center of the Union line. In response to Meade's warning, Warren tried to fill the gap with Crawford's division but lacked the troops to do so. Meade and Grant therefore ordered Hancock to remain on the plank road until noon of the following day, and then to withdraw east to the main Union line. This left Hancock and Gregg isolated west of Hatcher's Run and vulnerable to a Confederate attack.

Even as Union forces tried to turn the Confederate right flank, the rebel defenders there attempted to exploit the opportunity beyond Hatcher's Run. Illness once more compelled General Hill to relinquish command of the Confederate right to General Heth, his senior division commander. Heth's force consisted of his own four-brigade division and two brigades of Wilcox's division, as well as one cavalry brigade, all located north of Hancock's position. Hill also sent Mahone's division from Petersburg to bolster the rebel right, while cavalry under Hampton and Rooney Lee lurked to the west and southwest of the exposed II Corps.

About 1630, Mahone's division and an attached brigade crossed Hatcher's Run with about 5,000 men and attacked the II Corps' right flank, much to the surprise of Hancock and his men. At first, panic gripped some Federal regiments, and they fled into the tangled forest, but then Hancock counterattacked and drove Mahone's three brigades back across the stream. "The enemy became panic-stricken and gave way," reported a Union officer at the scene. Hampton's Confederate cavalry also pressured the II Corps from the west, but could make no headway against the Yankee infantry. Hancock later received permission from Grant to retreat from his vulnerable position that night, and by 0100 on 28 October, his exhausted men rejoined the other Union corps around Armstrong's Mill.

General Hancock
(Library of Congress)

"The attempt [to seize the Boydton Plank Road] was a failure," Grant wrote. He therefore "ordered the troops to withdraw, and they were all back in their former positions the next day." In the Battle of the Boydton Plank Road, the Federals sustained over 1,700 casualties, mostly from the II Corps, compared with 1,300 fallen rebels.

A comparative lull occurred after the action, known variously as the Battle of Hatcher's Run and the Battle of Burgess' Mill. After Wright's VI Corps returned from the Shenandoah, Grant decided to make another push. On 7 December, he sent Warren with 22,000 infantry from the V Corps and a II Corps division as well as 4,200 cavalry under Gregg to strike the Weldon Railroad. By the next day they were wrecking track as far south as Jarratt's Station, about thirty miles from Petersburg. Once aware of this expedition, Lee ordered Hampton's cavalry to pursue it, and then sent infantry under General Hill in support. On 9 December, the rebel troopers stopped Warren's progress at Hicksford, where they prevented the Federals from destroying a key railroad bridge across the Meherrin River. Pelted by sleet and freezing rain, the Federals marched back to Petersburg by

11 December, burning and looting as they went, having wrecked sixteen miles of track.

During the winter months, most of the Union and Confederate troops remained hunkered down in their cold, wet trenches. Because of a superior logistical network, the Federal soldiers generally ate better and wore warmer clothing than their Southern counterparts. At the end of 1864, Union forces in the Richmond–Petersburg theater numbered about 120,000 men. President Lincoln's re-election on 8 November meant that the North would fight on. Although the Confederate government sent emissaries to negotiate peace with the Lincoln administration in January 1865, these efforts came to naught, as did a second attempt by the South to broker an armistice aboard the *River Queen* at Hampton Roads on 3 February, attended by Lincoln and Confederate Vice President Alexander H. Stephens.

Meanwhile, Grant's armies underwent several significant leadership changes. General Hancock went on leave in November due to his unhealed Gettysburg wound, and would not return to the Army of the Potomac. In his place, Meade's capable chief of staff, Maj. Gen. Andrew A. Humphreys, assumed command of the II Corps. In December, the X and XVIII Corps were discontinued. The white divisions of the two organizations composed the new XXIV Corps under Maj. Gen. John Gibbon, and the black divisions became the XXV Corps under Weitzel, recently promoted to major general. In December, General Butler directed an unsuccessful campaign against Fort Fisher, near Wilmington, North Carolina. On 7 January 1865, Grant removed Butler from command of the Army of the James and replaced him with General Ord, now recovered from his Fort Harrison wound.

Within the Confederate army, food was scarce, pay was in arrears, and despondent men deserted by the thousands. Lee kept the remaining troops busy improving the thirty-seven miles of trenches around Petersburg and Richmond, but all their hard work could not disguise the fact that, by the end of January 1865, the Federals outnumbered his ragged army of 70,000 men by almost two to one. Recognizing the South's manpower shortage, on 13 March Confederate President Jefferson Davis signed into law an act allowing enlistments of black soldiers, if they had been emancipated by their masters. Few blacks enlisted, however, and the measure was ineffectual in bolstering the strength of the rebel armies.

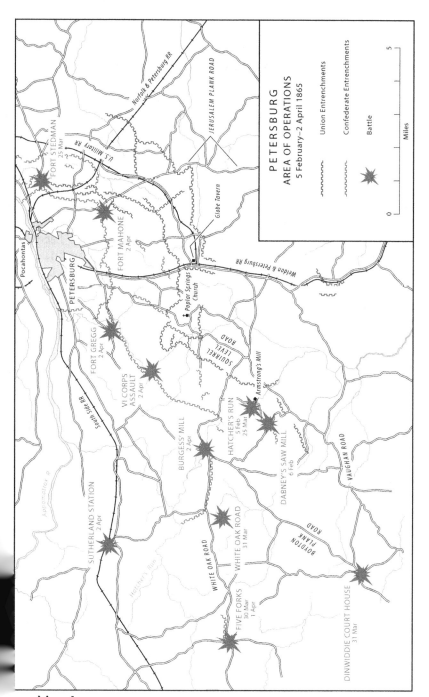

PETERSBURG
AREA OF OPERATIONS
5 February–2 April 1865

········· Union Entrenchments

ᴧᴧᴧᴧᴧ Confederate Entrenchments

✶ Battle

0 _____ 5
Miles

FORT STEDMAN
25 Mar

Norfolk & Petersburg RR

JERUSALEM PLANK ROAD

U.S. Military RR

Globe Tavern

FORT MAHONE
2 Apr

PETERSBURG

Pocahontas

Appomattox R.

Weldon & Petersburg RR

Poplar Springs Church

FORT GREGG
2 Apr

SQUIRREL LEVEL ROAD

Armstrong's Mill

VI CORPS ASSAULT
2 Apr

South Side RR

BURGESS' MILL
2 Apr

HATCHER'S RUN
5 Feb
25 Mar

DABNEY'S SAW MILL
6 Feb

VAUGHAN ROAD

SUTHERLAND STATION
2 Apr

Hatcher's Run

WHITE OAK ROAD
31 Mar

WHITE OAK ROAD

BOYDTON PLANK ROAD

FIVE FORKS
30 Mar
1 Apr

DINWIDDIE COURT HOUSE
31 Mar

MAP 4

Lee kept Longstreet and his First Corps north of the Appomattox River, including Field's and Maj. Gen. George E. Pickett's divisions. Kershaw's division returned to Longstreet in late November 1864 from campaigning with Early in the Shenandoah Valley. Kershaw was followed by the Army of Northern Virginia's Second Corps, which reached Petersburg in December, although Early himself remained in the Valley with a small force. Lee placed Maj. Gen. John B. Gordon in command of the Second Corps in Early's absence. General Hill still led the army's Third Corps on the right flank west of Petersburg, and General Ewell commanded Richmond's defensive force. Lee created a Fourth Corps in the fall, which he placed under General Anderson, but it consisted of only one division after Lee was compelled to send General Hoke's troops to North Carolina in late December to meet the Union threat to Fort Fisher. In January 1865, Lee also transferred one division of cavalry to South Carolina, and he reluctantly sent his cavalry commander, General Hampton, along with it. These sorely missed detachments would never return to the Army of Northern Virginia.

THE BATTLE OF HATCHER'S RUN

In February 1865, Grant renewed his effort to cut the Confederate supply routes into the city. Warren's foray against the Weldon Railroad in December had failed to prevent the rebels from using it and the Boydton Plank Road to transport supplies. At Grant's behest, Meade attempted to capture the road and the South Side Railroad with a 34,000-man strike force. On 5 February, Gregg's cavalry division rode west to attack the enemy's wagons moving on the Boydton Plank Road near Dinwiddie Court House and the Confederate right flank at Burgess' Mill. To prevent any danger to the cavalry from Hill's rebel infantry, Meade moved Warren's V Corps south of Hatcher's Run and sent it west on the Vaughan Road. At the same time, two II Corps divisions marched west from Globe Tavern on the north bank of Hatcher's Run to cover the V Corps' right—or northern—flank. The II Corps troops ran into the breastworks of Heth's rebel division in front of the Boydton Plank Road, halted, and then dug in near Armstrong's Mill, at a key crossing of Hatcher's Run (*See Map 4*).

About 1600, the divisions of Heth and Brig. Gen. Clement A. Evans (of Gordon's Second Corps) left the Petersburg trench lines and attacked Humphreys' II Corps bluecoats through the tangled

5th Corps, 7th of February, *by Alfred R. Waud*
(Library of Congress)

woods from the north, but were repulsed three times. That night, the V Corps moved closer to Humphreys' position by Armstrong's Mill, as did Gregg's troopers, who could find only eighteen Confederate supply wagons on the Boydton Plank Road to destroy.

On the afternoon of 6 February, Crawford's and Brig. Gen. Romeyn B. Ayres' V Corps divisions collided with the advancing Confederate divisions of Brig. Gen. John Pegram (Second Corps) and Mahone (Third Corps) at Dabney's Saw Mill, on the south side of Hatcher's Run. During the back-and-forth fighting around the mill and in the surrounding woods, Pegram was killed, but the Federals could make no further headway against the 14,000 Southern defenders, and many demoralized Union soldiers fled the field. "The musketry fire on both sides was for a time as terrible as any of the war," noted a veteran reporter who witnessed the battle. That night, the temperature plummeted, and snow and sleet fell on the soldiers, adding to their misery. On 7 February, after some inconclusive fighting, Meade ordered the Federals to dig in and extend their lines from Armstrong's Mill four miles eastward to integrate the newly dug fieldworks with the existing defenses. Although Meade had failed to gain the South Side Railroad, Union troops now stood only three miles from that important objective.

THE TIGHTENING NOOSE

Although Lee's lines of communications to the west were still intact, he recognized the dire situation his army faced. As the Union lines stretched farther west, the rebels could lengthen their own defenses only with difficulty, and in some sections of the trenches, Confederate soldiers already stood fifteen feet apart. A lack of supplies and rampant desertion remained critical problems, as did the deteriorating strategic situation. Union forces under Maj. Gen. William T. Sherman had captured Savannah, Georgia, in December 1864, and in January 1865, Fort Fisher fell to a second Federal expeditionary force under General Terry, closing Wilmington, the South's last remaining seaport. Wilmington itself fell to Terry's command on 22 February. Meanwhile, Sherman's 60,000 troops reached Columbia, the capital of South Carolina, on 17 February, and by the next morning, much of the city lay in ashes. A 15,000-man force led by Maj. Gen. John M. Schofield threatened inland North Carolina from New Bern, near the coast. Lee knew that Union success in the Carolinas would spell doom for his own diminishing army in Virginia, which relied on the lower South to provide food, fodder, and war materiel. He wished to "unite our armies, as separately they do not seem able to make head against the enemy." Lee also warned Confederate President Davis that "it may be necessary to abandon our cities" due to Sherman's advance and Grant's increasing pressure on Petersburg and Richmond.

On 6 February, Davis appointed Lee general in chief of all Confederate forces, although the general's ability to direct the rebel armies by that time was limited. Two weeks later, at Lee's request, the Confederate War Department appointed General Joseph E. Johnston to lead all rebel troops in the Carolinas, primarily to prevent Sherman from uniting with Schofield and Terry, and then marching northward to join Grant. Lee and Davis knew that if Sherman's army group combined with Federal forces in Virginia all would be lost. Lee began to consider abandoning Petersburg and uniting with Johnston's army to defeat Sherman and Grant separately.

In early March, however, Lee received the distressing news that Sheridan had crushed Early in the upper Shenandoah Valley, cutting off one of the rebels' major supply sources, and freeing an additional 20,000 Federal troops for action at Richmond and Petersburg. Since the Davis administration refused to consider a political settlement that did not grant Confederate independence—rendering a negotiated end to the war highly improbable—Lee decided to attempt a breakout against Grant's formidable siege lines. In the meantime, he

Interior of Fort Stedman
(Library of Congress)

warned Davis that the fall of the Confederate capital was growing more likely with each passing day.

ATTACK ON FORT STEDMAN

For several weeks in March, Lee conferred with General Gordon, the Second Corps commander, about the possibility of an assault on Union lines. Lee hoped that if part of his army captured a section of Meade's fortifications Grant would constrict his lengthy siege lines around Petersburg, which might enable Lee to defend the city with fewer men. If so, Lee could then send some troops to unite with Johnson's army and defeat Sherman. The need for an assault at Petersburg was made more pressing by the junction of Sherman's army group with Schofield's 30,000-man force (now including Terry's corps) at Goldsboro, North Carolina, on 23 March, along with signs that Grant intended to strike Lee's right flank.

Gordon recommended that a Confederate assault be made against Fort Stedman, located 150 yards from the rebel lines between the crater and the Appomattox River. The three-quarters-acre fort stood within the IX Corps' sector and was badly deteriorated owing to its constant exposure to Confederate fire. The fort was vulnerable to attack, having no bastions and just four cannons. It also stood close to the City Point Railroad, the capture of which would put the Confederates in a position to threaten the main Union supply depot and Grant's headquarters. Lee assumed that Grant would then shift troops from his left to counter the rebel threat, which was Lee's main objective. Gordon maintained that such a blow would cripple the Union army around the city, "or at least . . . disable it temporarily, enabling us to withdraw from Petersburg in safety and join Johnston in North Carolina."

To increase the chances of success, Lee ordered Gordon to command the effort, spearheaded by his own Second Corps troops, and reinforced by several brigades from Anderson's and Hill's corps, as well as one brigade of cavalry. From north of the James, Pickett's division of Longstreet's corps was also included in the attack plan, but Lee was doubtful that Pickett's men could reach the point of the attack in time to be of service. Gordon planned to launch his surprise assault before dawn, and after capturing Fort Stedman and its supporting batteries, have his infantry expand the attack north and south along the Union line, while the cavalry wreaked havoc in the Federal rear.

Gordon's well-planned operation began at 0400 on 25 March, quickly overrunning Fort Stedman and capturing the flanking batteries as well, "after a brief but gallant resistance," a Union officer reported. But the Union defenders soon recovered from the shock of the onslaught, and several adjacent Federal batteries began to pound the Confederates with a deadly crossfire. In the meantime, Gordon's attack started to unravel. The expected rebel cavalry never materialized, some of Gordon's infantry units became disoriented while negotiating the labyrinthine Union trenches in the darkness, and many hungry rebels found the abandoned Federal rations too tempting to ignore. As a result, Gordon's attack ground to a halt as the Confederates collided with determined IX Corps infantry. Realizing that the earthworks beyond Fort Stedman "could only be taken at great sacrifice," Lee authorized Gordon to pull his men back to the main rebel line at 0800. Rather than risk being shot in the back during the retreat, hundreds of Confederates surrendered to the Federals. Gordon's attack on Fort Stedman resulted in about 2,700 Southern casualties, while the Union IX Corps lost 1,044. "It was a desperate military gamble," one of Grant's staff officers concluded, "with very few chances of winning." Suspecting that Lee had weakened his right flank in order to make the assault, Union II and VI Corps troops attacked that afternoon along Hatcher's Run, netting another 800 rebel prisoners, while incurring heavy losses of their own.

FINAL BATTLES AROUND PETERSBURG

Lee's last offensive had failed and had cost him almost one-tenth of his force defending Petersburg. Moreover, it was a crushing blow to Southern morale. Lee's men had "lost hope of final success, and the men were not willing to risk their lives in a hopeless endeavor," concluded one Confederate officer at Petersburg. The day after the attack on Fort Stedman, the Southern commander warned President Davis that it would now "be impossible to prevent a junction between Grant and Sherman," and he advised against his army remaining at Richmond and Petersburg until the arrival of Sherman's army group. Lee knew—as did Grant—that his 60,000 troops could not remain in place if the Federals cut the South Side Railroad near Hatcher's Run. But Lee needed time to prepare his army for the effort to join Johnston's small force in North Carolina. The Confederate crisis was exacerbated by the arrival in late March of General Sheridan and his Union cavalry corps from the Shenandoah Valley. The Federal mobile strike force, Lee understood, would soon spell trouble for his vulnerable right flank and the supply lines it protected.

On 27 March, Grant met with Sherman at his City Point headquarters, the latter having just arrived by steamship from North Carolina. That evening, the two generals called on President Lincoln, who had sailed down from Washington, and on the following day, they were joined by Rear Adm. David D. Porter, commander of the U.S. Navy's North Atlantic Blockading Squadron. During the meeting, the Northern leaders discussed military strategy and Lincoln's plans for restoring the nation once the rebellion was crushed and the Southern armed forces had surrendered. The president favored a conciliatory approach—"I want submission and no more bloodshed," he firmly stated. Lincoln hoped another battle could be avoided, and when the time came,

The Peacemakers (detail), *by George Peter Alexander Healy*
(The White House Historical Association)

he urged the generals to give the surrendering Confederates "the most liberal and honorable of terms." Sherman soon returned to his command in North Carolina, where he would pursue Johnston's heavily outnumbered army. Grant, meanwhile, prepared to launch what he hoped would be his last campaign against Lee.

Although Sherman had urged Grant to postpone an attack on Lee's lines until his Federal forces in North Carolina could reach Petersburg, Grant feared the possibility that "Lee should get away some night before I was aware of it, and having the lead of me, push into North Carolina to join with Johnston." The Union general in chief accordingly readied his forces for renewed operations against Lee's army. Several days before Gordon's attack on Fort Stedman, Grant had ordered his army and corps commanders to be ready to move on 29 March. General Ord was to shift 16,000 men from his Army of the James to the far left of the Union defenses south of Petersburg, leaving 14,000 troops under General Weitzel at Bermuda Hundred and Deep Bottom. Parke's IX Corps and Wright's VI Corps remained in the lines before Petersburg with about 35,000 troops, prepared to punch through the rebel defenses if weakened by Lee to meet the threat on his right. Grant ordered Humphrey's II Corps and Warren's V Corps "to get into a position from which we could strike the South Side Railroad and ultimately the Danville Railroad" west of Petersburg once Ord's troops had replaced them in the trenches. While Warren's and Humphreys' infantry crossed Hatcher's Run and advanced on the Confederate right flank, Sheridan and his 13,000 troopers were to seize a strategic road junction on Lee's far western flank called Five Forks, and then strike Lee's remaining supply lines in the enemy's rear.

General Meade accompanied the 35,000 soldiers of the II and V Corps, hoping to be present when they captured the Boydton Plank Road, one of the Confederates' few remaining supply routes to Petersburg. Sheridan, meanwhile, began his movement in a heavy rain on 29 March. He started from near Globe Tavern and rode southwest to Dinwiddie Court House, arriving there at 1700. The next day, Sheridan advanced some of his troopers north toward Five Forks over muddy roads, but they fell back to Dinwiddie Court House in the face of stiff resistance from rebel cavalry. Warned of the new threat to his right, Lee had posted a force at Five Forks consisting of Pickett's 5,000-man infantry division and 5,500 troopers under his nephew, Fitzhugh Lee.

With the major turning movement well underway, Grant decided to modify the Union forces' objectives. He ordered Sheridan to make Lee's army his main focus. "I do not want you . . . to cut loose and go after the enemy's [rail]roads at present," Grant told Sheridan, but instead, "in the morning, push around the enemy, if you can, and get on his right rear." To bolster Sheridan's mounted force for the offensive, Grant placed the V Corps under the cavalry-man's orders, although Sheridan had requested the VI Corps, which he had commanded in the recent Shenandoah Valley Campaign.

The next day, Warren's rain-soaked V Corps approached the Confederate position along White Oak Road, an east-west route from Burgess' Mill to Five Forks, along which Anderson's Fourth Corps had established a line of fieldworks. After initially pushing back rebel forces south of the road, Warren's advancing troops passed through heavily wooded terrain, where Bushrod Johnson's Confederate division struck them hard on the left flank. Many of the Federal units dissolved in chaos. "Brigade after brigade broke," recalled a Union officer, and "that strange impulse termed a 'panic' took effect and the retreat became a rout." Later, fresh V Corps troops managed to take back much of the lost ground and push Johnson's rebels back to the White Oak Road, but the heavy fighting delayed Warren's junction with Sheridan.

While the battle raged near the White Oak Road, Sheridan was hard-pressed to hold on to Dinwiddie Court House against the onslaught from Pickett's foot soldiers and Fitzhugh Lee's cavalry. But Brig. Gen. George A. Custer's division of Union troopers, armed with Spencer repeating carbines, poured out "such a shower of lead that nothing could stand up against it," and then launched a dismounted charge, which thwarted the rebels' advance toward the courthouse.

Once Pickett learned that V Corps troops had moved nearby, he returned north to Five Forks early on the morning of 1 April. Pickett's men dug in there along the White Oak Road. They were supported by Rooney Lee's cavalry and several batteries of artillery. Lee ordered Pickett to hold the crossroads "at all hazards," as the loss of the key intersection on the extreme Confederate right would enable Sheridan's cavalry to seize the South Side Railroad three miles to the north, cutting Lee's last supply line.

On 1 April, Sheridan moved his cavalry and the V Corps north from Dinwiddie Court House toward Five Forks, and he was "exceedingly anxious to attack at once." Upon nearing the junction, he dismounted his cavalry and sent them forward to pin down Pickett's forces in his front, and then directed Warren to begin his infantry attack on the rebel position from the Union right— or eastern—flank. Slowed by muddy roads and heavily wooded terrain, Warren's attack began shortly after 1600—a lengthy delay that would ultimately cost him his command. But when the Federals struck, they struck hard. Ayres' V Corps division hammered the enemy's left flank with overwhelming force, the attacking blue-coats urged on by Sheridan, who rode at the front of Warren's surging line. Advancing undetected through tangled woods, Crawford's and Brig. Gen. Charles Griffin's divisions outflanked Pickett's line and secured Ford's Road in the Confederate rear, giving them a clear path to the South Side Railroad. In the ensuing rout, the victorious V Corps troops rounded up thousands of rebel prisoners, while the remaining Confederates fled northwest, away from Petersburg.

By 1830, Pickett's shattered command was in full retreat. "The cowardly ran, the timid were dumbfounded, the brave, alone, could not withstand the vastly superior force of the enemy," wrote one wounded rebel. Sheridan's success was due in part to Pickett's absence from the field during most of the battle. He had been enjoying a shad bake with Fitzhugh Lee two miles north of Five Forks when the fighting began and arrived on the battlefield too late to affect the outcome.

Map of the Battle of Five Forks
(Library of Congress)

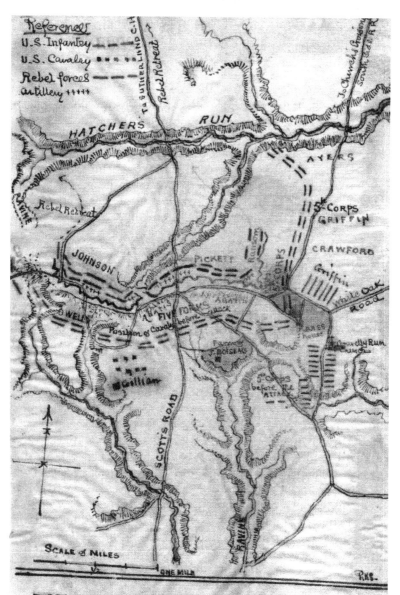

Although victorious, Sheridan was enraged at Warren for what the cavalryman regarded as inexcusable slowness in carrying out his orders. With Grant's authorization, he relieved Warren of command and replaced him with General Griffin, the V Corps' senior division commander. The Battle of Five Forks cost the Confederates roughly 3,000 casualties compared with the Federals' 830 losses.

With Sheridan's victory, the rebel lines at Petersburg were broken on the right, and the South Side Railroad could no longer be defended. Worse yet, Lee's best escape route to Johnston's army was now blocked. To meet this crisis, Lee ordered Longstreet to hurry to Petersburg with one of his divisions from Richmond. The rebels also abandoned three miles of entrenchments on their western flank, lacking the soldiers to occupy the positions. Lee knew that he had to shore up his right flank at Petersburg to buy enough time for his army's withdrawal from the two besieged cities.

Upon hearing the news of the Union victory at Five Forks, Grant ordered an assault on the rebel lines around Petersburg for the morning of 2 April, to be preceded by a three-hour artillery bombardment the night before. From their positions around Fort Sedgwick on the Jerusalem Turnpike, IX Corps units surged north at 0430 to hit Gordon's Second Corps Confederates. In obedience to orders, General Parke directed the assault, though he had little confidence in the operation's success. The fighting was fierce in the maze of trenches and rifle pits south of Petersburg, particularly around Fort Mahone, but the stubborn enemy defenders managed to turn back the Federal onslaught by midafternoon.

Also on 2 April, about 0445, Wright's VI Corps attacked the thinly defended rebel earthworks of A. P. Hill's corps "with the utmost gallantry and determination" from positions facing Fort Welch and Fort Gregg, west of Globe Tavern and the Weldon Railroad. Wright had deployed his 14,000 troops in columns close to the rebel trenches, and within thirty minutes, the densely packed Union formations punched a gaping hole in Lee's thin lines, allowing thousands of VI Corps soldiers to race toward the Boydton Plank Road and the South Side Railroad while the rebel defenders fled or surrendered. "It was a hard fought battle," wrote one Massachusetts soldier, "but it brought brilliant success, though with a terrible cost."

In the aftermath of their success, Wright's troops were thoroughly disorganized, having suffered some 2,200 casualties in the assault. Many Federals reached the Boydton Plank Road, while others advanced to the long-sought-after South Side Railroad. Most of Wright's troops, however, wheeled left after they had breached the enemy lines. Then they rushed along the rear of the rebel positions toward Burgess' Mill, "sweeping everything before them," Grant later reported. With help from the II Corps, they succeeded in prying Heth's troops out of their trenches along Hatcher's Run and pursued them northward for two miles to Sutherland Station on the South Side Railroad. Here four Confederate brigades made a stand against Brig. Gen. Nelson A. Miles' II Corps division, but they were routed by a Union flank attack and forced to flee northwest to the Appomattox River, the Federals capturing 1,000 of the rebels. Miles' troops were too disorganized and exhausted to pursue the fleeing enemy, but the South Side Railroad, Lee's last supply line, was now firmly in Union control.

Breastworks of the Confederate Fort Mahone
(Library of Congress)

THE FALL OF RICHMOND

The Confederate high command recognized the danger that Wright's breakthrough presented, and Lee and Longstreet could

clearly see the advancing Federal formations from Lee's headquar
ters west of Petersburg. The Union juggernaut had thrown back
five Southern brigades and had taken four miles of defensive line
stretching from the western outskirts of the city to Hatcher's Run.
In the mêlée that followed, General Hill rashly rode along the
Boydton Plank Road to assess the situation and was killed by a
Union soldier from the VI Corps. To shore up his position, Lee
gathered troops west of the city in defenses along Indian Town
Creek, with two small rebel forts—Gregg and Whitworth—situated
in advance of the line. He hoped to use these earthen defenses
to stall the Union attack and enable his hard-pressed soldiers to
withdraw from Petersburg later that day. Knowing that the fall of
the Confederate capital was at hand, on the morning of 2 April,
Lee notified Confederate Secretary of War John C. Breckinridge
and President Davis that Petersburg and Richmond would have to
be evacuated by nightfall. "It is absolutely necessary that we should
abandon our position tonight, or run the risk of being cut off in the
morning," Lee glumly advised his civilian superiors.

Lee was correct to anticipate an attack on the Indian Town
Creek line. After Wright's corps had overrun Hill's entrenched
troops at dawn on 2 April, Gibbon's relatively fresh XXIV Corps
from the Army of the James moved north into the breach, and
at 1300, launched an attack against the last Confederate line
astride the Boydton Plank Road. The outnumbered Southern
defenders of Fort Gregg mounted a stout defense against Gibbon's
onrushing Yankees, but the fort was overwhelmed after what one
Confederate called a "desperate hand-to-hand conflict." General
Grant, who witnessed Gibbon's attack, immediately ordered all
Union commands to assault Lee's weakened positions. Grant's
attack order even included the II and VI Corps, who had to hurry
back to Petersburg from Hatcher's Run. Lee thwarted further
Union penetrations of his lines with a 4,600-man reinforcement
from Longstreet's First Corps, which had made a rapid march
from Richmond and had taken position east of the two fallen forts.
Lee now hoped to hold on to the city until nightfall, when he could
extricate his much-reduced forces and move west.

While Federal troops from the Army of the Potomac and
the Army of the James battled the main Confederate army at
Petersburg, rebels in Anderson's corps, Fitzhugh Lee's cavalry, and
the infantry divisions of Heth, Pickett, and Johnson were cut off
from their comrades in gray by the II and VI Corps troops west

of the city. By midafternoon, these Confederate formations under Anderson's overall command moved northwest on the south side of the Appomattox River toward an eventual junction with Lee, closely pursued by Union cavalry.

Having advised the civilian authorities to evacuate Richmond, Lee began to withdraw the rest of his army from the two cities on the evening of 2 April. "It will be a difficult operation," Lee wrote, "but I hope not impracticable." The immediate objective of the Army of Northern Virginia was to reach Amelia Court House on the Richmond and Danville Railroad, thirty-six miles northwest of Petersburg. There, Lee was informed, food and other supplies would be waiting for his retreating army, which would then march south to join General Johnston's forces in North Carolina. Taking most of their field artillery and hundreds of wagons with them, Longstreet and Gordon withdrew from the Petersburg lines and crossed the Appomattox River, heading west toward Amelia. Mahone's forces guarding the Richmond and Petersburg Railroad at Bermuda Hundred also retreated west, as did Ewell's two divisions defending Richmond, much of which was burned by Confederate authorities and looters during the evacuation.

Early on the morning of 3 April, Union troops crossed the deserted rebel earthworks and entered Petersburg, while twenty-odd miles to the north, Richmond mayor Joseph C. Mayo surrendered the city to Union forces under General Weitzel. After almost four years of devastating civil war, U.S. forces at last occupied the rebel capital and main logistical hub. That evening, Lincoln telegraphed his congratulations to Grant from City Point: "Allow me to tender to you and all with you the nation's grateful thanks." On 4 April, Lincoln and his son Tad entered Richmond, and were recognized by many former slaves, who jubilantly greeted the president. "No electric wire could have carried the news of the President's arrival sooner than it was circulated through Richmond," wrote Admiral Porter, who accompanied Lincoln, "They all wanted to shake hands with Mr. Lincoln or his coat tail or even to kneel down and kiss his boots!" Lincoln's party toured Jefferson Davis' official residence, the Virginia state capitol, and a former military prison.

Retreat to the West

In order to shorten the marching columns, Lee's forces made their way west to Amelia Court House by several routes. The army's wagon train took the most northerly route via Powhatan Court

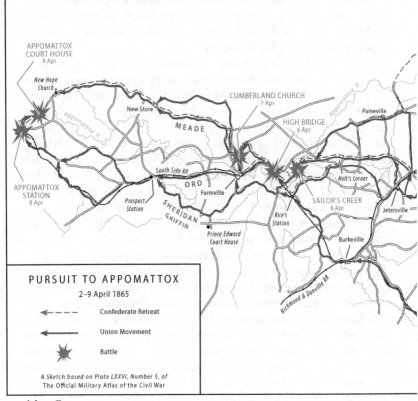

APPOMATTOX
COURT HOUSE
9 Apr

New Hope
Church

New Store

CUMBERLAND CHURCH
7 Apr

Paineville

MEADE

HIGH BRIDGE
6 Apr

Appomattox R.

South Side RR

ORD

Farmville

Holt's Corner

APPOMATTOX
STATION
8 Apr

Prospect
Station

SHERIDAN
GRIFFIN

SAILOR'S CREEK
6 Apr

Jetersville

Rice's
Station

Prince Edward
Court House

Burkeville

Richmond & Danville RR

PURSUIT TO APPOMATTOX
2–9 April 1865

← – – – Confederate Retreat

← Union Movement

✸ Battle

A Sketch based on Plate LXXVI, Number 5, of
The Official Military Atlas of the Civil War

MAP 5

House, while most of the troops crossed the Appomattox River at
Goode's Bridge, and then reached Amelia on 4 April. They were
joined by Fitzhugh Lee's cavalry and the infantry divisions under
Anderson that had been cut off from Petersburg after the battles
of Five Forks and Sutherland Station. During Anderson's retreat,
elements of Custer's Union cavalry division struck the rear of the
Confederate column at Namozine Church south of the Appomattox
River on 3 April, but the rebels were able to continue their hasty
retreat. During the pursuit, "hundreds and hundreds of prisoners,
armed and unarmed, fell into our hands," Sheridan noted (*Map 5*).

In the meantime, the Confederates arriving at Amelia Court
House received a severe shock. Although Lee had directed that provi-

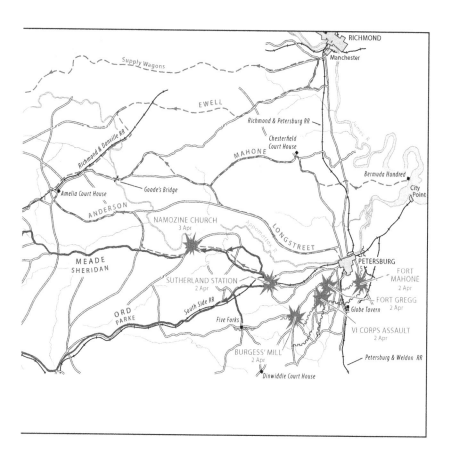

sions for his army be sent there, his staff found only train cars loaded with ammunition, not the rations they had expected and that Lee's famished troops sorely needed. In fact, millions of rations intended for Lee's army were not shipped and still lay in warehouses at Lynchburg and Danville, and Greensboro, North Carolina; nor did the 350,000 rations from Richmond arrive as Lee expected. The army's commissary officers had no choice but to forage on the surrounding countryside, but this expedient met with little success, given the sparsely settled region they were passing through. Meanwhile, discipline began to break down, and desertions increased. One rebel noted that some soldiers "wandered off in search of food," while others "followed the example of the [Confederate] government and fled." As

Lee well knew, the precious time spent gathering provisions allowed the pursuing Federals to draw ever closer to his waiting army. The Confederate commander telegraphed commissaries in Danville to send all rations by rail to Jetersville eight miles southwest of Amelia Court House, and he planned to march there on the following day while en route to Danville. Moreover, Ewell's troops from Richmond were slow to reach Amelia, as were the army's wagons, which further delayed Lee's progress.

Before entering Petersburg on 3 April, Grant had ordered Union forces to pursue Lee south of the Appomattox River. General Ord's Army of the James moved west along the South Side Railroad, followed by Parke's IX Corps, heading for the important rail junction of Burkeville, a fifty-mile march. After meeting with Lincoln briefly at Petersburg, Grant accompanied this column, heading west to Sutherland Station on the night of the third. Between this column and the river, Meade led the II, V, and VI Corps of the Army of the Potomac, with Sheridan's two cavalry divisions in the van. Roughly 80,000 Federals chased Lee's fleeing army. "The pursuit had now become swift, unflagging, relentless," one of Grant's staff noted. The bluecoats sought to remain south of Lee's retreating columns to prevent the enemy's link up with Johnston in North Carolina. "We did not want to follow [Lee]," Grant explained, "we wanted to get ahead of him and cut him off."

Sheridan's cavalry and Griffin's V Corps infantry reached Jetersville on 4 April and dug in across the railroad south of town. Grant ordered Meade to reinforce Sheridan with the rest of his army, while to the south, Ord and Parke continued their westward march to Burkeville, with the IX Corps repairing the South Side Railroad and guarding the supply wagons.

On 5 April, Sheridan sent out a brigade of cavalry under Brig. Gen. Henry E. Davies Jr. to the north in search of the enemy. Davies' men destroyed a train of 200 rebel supply wagons at Paineville, ten miles northwest of Amelia Court House, before returning to Jetersville, pursued by most of Fitzhugh Lee's cavalry. That afternoon, Lee's army continued its southwesterly march from Amelia Court House, but stopped short of Jetersville when Sheridan's cavalry came into view. Much to the Confederates' disappointment, Sheridan's mounted force was soon strengthened by arriving II and VI Corps infantry units.

Sheridan believed that Lee would move west, now that the road to Danville was blocked. Meade, however, thought that Lee would concentrate at Amelia Court House, and began preparing to advance against the rebels from the east and south. Adamant in his convictions, Sheridan sent a message to Grant, imploring him to come to Jetersville. Before setting out to find Sheridan and Meade, Grant "gave Ord directions to continue his march to Burkeville and there intrench himself for the night." The next morning, Ord was to move farther west "to cut off all the roads between there and Farmville," which was located fifteen miles to the northwest on Lee's probable route of march. Riding with a small escort, Grant arrived at Jetersville late on 5 April, and conferred with Meade and Sheridan. All agreed to an advance against Lee from Jetersville in the morning.

Attack on the Rear Guard, Amelia Court House, *by Alfred R. Waud*
(Library of Congress)

THE BATTLE OF SAILOR'S CREEK

General Lee, of course, developed his own plans that night. Rather than assail the enemy's entrenched line blocking the road to Jetersville, he decided to move his army beyond Sheridan's left flank toward Farmville, about twenty miles to the west, where he expected to find rations. Marching toward Rice's Station on the South Side Railroad, Longstreet led both the Confederate First and Third Corps, with the troops of Anderson, Ewell, and Gordon following him on a single road. At times the rear of Lee's column came within sight of the Union pursuers, "in this great race, neck and neck," as a Federal officer described it. Although Longstreet's command and three divisions of Hill's former corps reached Rice's Station early on 6 April, the rest of Lee's army had to fend off repeated attacks from Sheridan's aggressive Federal cavalry units that morning. When Confederate troops in the rear of the column failed to arrive at Rice's Station, Lee grew concerned for their safety.

The Surrender of Ewell's Corps at Sailor's Creek, *by Alfred R. Waud*
(Library of Congress)

The Confederate commander had good reason to worry. On the morning of 6 April, Sheridan's cavalrymen rode west from Jetersville on a route parallel to Lee's, several miles to the south. Meade's three infantry corps found that the enemy had departed the Amelia Court House area the previous night, so the II, V, and VI Corps turned west in pursuit. Near a crossroads called Holt's Corner, Union cavalry attacked Anderson's corps in what Grant described as "a severe engagement." Although repulsed, the blue-coats forced Anderson to halt his march and deploy for battle. Sheridan exploited the situation by rushing mounted units into the gap that had formed between Anderson's stationary line and Longstreet's marching column, thereby cutting off Anderson's command from the Confederate main body.

Behind Anderson, Ewell feared for the safety of Lee's wagon train, given the ongoing Union cavalry attacks and the Federal infantry closing in on the rear of the column. At Holt's Corner, he directed the wagons to use the Jamestown Road north of Rice's

Station Road, the Confederates' main retreat route. Gordon's Second Corps troops followed the wagons, with Humphreys' II Corps Federals in close pursuit. Meanwhile, on the main road, Ewell took up a defensive position on the west bank of Sailor's Creek, with Anderson's corps on the road ahead of him to the west. Wright's VI Corps soldiers soon reached the east bank of the creek, confronting Ewell's rebels.

After a half-hour cannonade by massed Union artillery, at 1800 on 6 April, Wright's 7,000 infantrymen attacked Ewell's command across a flooded Sailor's Creek from their positions near the Hillsman farm. The Union attackers overcame stiff enemy resistance and overwhelmed both of Ewell's flanks, capturing 3,400 fleeing rebels, including Ewell, Kershaw, and Maj. Gen. George Washington Custis Lee, the Confederate commander's eldest son. The situation on Anderson's front proved no better. The three Federal cavalry divisions under Custer, Maj. Gen. George Crook, and Brig. Gen. Thomas C. Devin struck hard, scattering Pickett's and Johnson's troops along the rebel center and left flank on Rice's Station Road. About 2,600 of Anderson's men were killed, wounded, or captured during the rout. "My God," Lee exclaimed in anguish as he watched his soldiers running from the field, "has the army dissolved?"

While Ewell's and Anderson's commands disintegrated, two miles to the north, Humphreys' Federals caught up with Gordon's corps and the Confederate supply wagons on the Lockett farm. A bottleneck had formed there, as Lee's slow-moving wagon train crossed two narrow bridges over Sailor's Creek. In the meantime, Gordon's men deployed on a ridge to the east to hold off Union pursuit until the wagons could get across. Attacking with two divisions of the VI Corps, Humphreys forced the rebels off the high ground and across the creek, capturing hundreds of wagons along with about 2,000 of Gordon's troops. In the fighting along Sailor's Creek, Lee lost almost 8,000 men, a crippling blow to an already depleted army.

MARCHING TO APPOMATTOX

Late on 6 April, after Longstreet's men had brushed off an attack at Rice's Station by troops of Gibbon's XXIV Corps, Lee began moving his army to Farmville, where a stockpile of provisions awaited. Longstreet's troops marched south of the Appomattox River, while General Mahone, now commanding the remnant of Anderson's corps, and the survivors of Gordon's Second Corps marched to Farmville along the South Side Railroad via High Bridge on the Appomattox, several miles east of town. Measuring 2,500 feet long, the railroad bridge rested on twenty-one brick piers. Below it, a more modest wooden wagon bridge spanned the river. On 6 April, a small Union force from Ord's Army of the James attempted to capture the bridge but was defeated by Southern cavalry and lost 800 men captured. The next day, the Confederate rear guard burned a section of the railroad bridge to delay pursuing Union forces, but were driven off by Federal troops of Brig. Gen. Francis C. Barlow's II Corps division before they could destroy the wagon bridge. Resuming the westward retreat, most of Lee's army reached the vicinity of Farmville on 7 April.

High Bridge crossing the Appomattox, near Farmville, on South Side Railroad
(Library of Congress)

Lee hoped to buy time to rest and feed his weary and diminishing army by placing the Appomattox River between his troops and the pursuing Federals, but Grant continued to push his lieutenants to close up on the retreating rebels and cut them off from the west. "To bring Lee's army to a stand was now the supreme object of every officer, high or low, and of every soldier in the ranks," a II Corps officer wrote. To the south, Griffin's V Corps and two of Sheridan's cavalry divisions marched on 7 April to Prince Edward Court House, and then pressed on toward Prospect Station on the South Side Railroad west of Farmville, to prevent Lee from making a sudden dash into North Carolina. North of Sheridan and Griffin, but still below the Appomattox River, General Ord pushed his Army of the James from Farmville along the rail line toward Prospect Station. At Prince Edward Court House, Sheridan learned that "seven trains of provisions and forage were at Appomattox," a station on the South Side Railroad about twenty-five miles to the west. The Union cavalryman informed Grant that he "determined to start at once and capture them, and a forced march was necessary in order to get there before Lee's army could secure them."

At Farmville on 7 April, the Federal II and VI Corps pressed Lee's hungry soldiers, and Crook's cavalry division attacked Confederate supply wagons filled with provisions. Some Southern troops reached the town, only to discover that approaching Union forces now prevented them from drawing their desperately needed rations. In danger of being surrounded, the Confederates had to move north across the river, burning the bridges behind them. No sooner had the Southern soldiers crossed than they had to face more pursuing bluecoats coming from the east.

Advancing from the High Bridge area, about 1400, Humphreys' II Corps troops encountered most of Lee's infantry entrenched on elevated ground at Cumberland Church, three miles north of Farmville. Humphreys attacked the enemy position twice from the east and north, and nearly turned the rebels' left flank under Mahone, but the Southern troops, supported by artillery, repulsed the Federal assaults. Union VI Corps reinforcements from Farmville could not be brought up in time for Humphreys to dislodge the rebels before dark, due to the damaged bridges over the Appomattox River. The fighting at Cumberland Church cost the Federals 655 casualties, including Brig. Gen. Thomas Smyth, a II Corps division commander who fell mortally wounded and died two days later—the last Union general killed in the war. The Confederate losses numbered about 255.

Lee's veterans continued their retreat at midnight, with many of the soldiers dropping out of the column from hunger, exhaustion, and despair. The once indomitable Army of Northern Virginia, Grant recalled, "was rapidly crumbling." Longstreet likewise noted that "the troops of our broken columns were troubled and faint of heart," while many of the rebels' mules and horses were too weak to pull wagons and cannons. Lee planned to resupply his men at Appomattox Station and then proceed west about twenty miles to Campbell Court House (present-day Rustburg), located eleven miles south of Lynchburg. From there, the Southern commander would proceed to Danville, another sixty miles to the south, en route to Johnston's army in North Carolina.

Prior to leaving Cumberland Church, Lee received a message from Grant late on the night of 7 April, in which the Union commanding general called on Lee to surrender his army and avoid "any further effusion of blood." In reply, Lee requested Grant's terms of capitulation, though he denied the "hopelessness of further resistance on the part of the Army of Northern Virginia." That night, Lee withdrew his army from the Cumberland Church line and headed west on several roads toward Appomattox Station via New Store, briefly halting at the latter point on the morning of 8 April. From New Store, Lee's army marched in a single column on the Richmond-Lynchburg Stage Road, with Gordon's command in the advance and Longstreet's force bringing up the rear.

Wright's and Humphreys' Federal corps under Meade followed close on Lee's heels north of the Appomattox River. Grant, who was "suffering very severely with a sick headache," accompanied Meade's column. Meanwhile, south of the river, Sheridan continued to push toward Appomattox Station with his troopers, followed by Ord's Army of the James and Griffin's V Corps. Moving "with alacrity and without any straggling," Grant reported, Sheridan's cavalry reached their destination on the afternoon of 8 April. Soon after their arrival, Custer's division managed to capture four supply trains, along with twenty-five guns, after driving away the surprised Confederate defenders. More importantly, a strong force of Union cavalry now blocked Lee's access to his supplies and the main road west.

On 8 April, Grant replied to Lee's note of the previous night. He informed the Confederate commander that with regard to terms, "there is but one condition I would insist upon—namely, that the men and officers surrendered shall be disqualified for taking up arms against the Government of the United States until properly exchanged." Grant also advised Lee of his willingness to meet "at any point agreeable to you."

The rest of the day saw the two belligerents continue moving west toward Appomattox Station, but with little fighting along the way. Lee's men arrived around the village of Appomattox Court House, five miles east of the rail depot. Late that night, Grant received a letter from Lee, in which the latter stated that he did "not think the emergency has arisen to call for the surrender of this army." Nevertheless, Lee did seek to bring an end to the fighting, and he suggested that they meet the following day at 1000 to discuss "the restoration of peace." Grant and his staff thought that Lee had changed his tune, and now sought a political settlement that stopped short of outright surrender. Perhaps Lee hoped to buy time in order to reach Johnston in North Carolina. These considerations mattered little to Grant, however, for he lacked the authority to conduct peace negotiations with Lee. More importantly, the Union general in chief also knew that he had the rebels all but cornered at Appomattox.

After a sleepless night, Grant began Palm Sunday, 9 April, by writing a reply to Lee, advising his Confederate counterpart that because he could not negotiate a peace, the proposed 1000 meeting "could lead to no good." The Union commander reiterated his desire to end hostilities, and he reminded Lee that "by the South laying down their arms they will hasten that most desirable event." Even as Grant wrote, Union forces were hastening the end of the war. While Sheridan blocked Lee's path to Appomattox Station and the desperately needed supply stores there, Ord and Griffin were hurrying to support the Union cavalryman. Grant and his staff left Meade's camp at New Store and rode south to join Sheridan's cavalry across the river, while two corps of infantry under Wright and Humphreys continued to press the rear of Lee's rapidly shrinking column.

On the morning of 9 April, Lee made one last attempt to break through the Union forces encircling his army. The Federals' capture of Appomattox Station meant that Lee would have to continue moving west to obtain supplies, and that Sheridan's troopers had to be pushed off the Stage Road. At 0750, Gordon's infantry and 2,400 rebel horsemen attacked Union cavalry units just west of Appomattox Court House in a sweeping advance to the southwest. At first, Gordon's attack succeeded in driving back the Federal troopers and opening the road, but infantry reinforcements from the V, XXIV, and XXV Corps, supported by Custer's and Devin's cavalry divisions, drove the attackers back toward the village. Some Confederate cavalry units under Fitzhugh Lee escaped to Lynchburg, but the rest of Lee's army was now surrounded. "There is nothing left for me to do but go and see General Grant," Lee told his staff upon hearing of Gordon's repulse.

Having crossed to the south side of the Appomattox River at Cutbank Ford, Grant received a letter from General Lee just before 1200 requesting an interview to discuss surrender terms. Grant notified Lee that he would "push forward to the front for the purpose of meeting you." Generals Gordon and Sheridan, meanwhile, arranged a cease-fire, despite the pugnacious Sheridan's eagerness to attack Lee and force his "absolute surrender by capture." When apprised of the cease-fire, Meade likewise halted the fighting along his lines near New Hope Church, about two miles east of Appomattox Court House.

THE SURRENDER

As the guns fell silent along the tense battle lines, Lee and Grant headed to Appomattox Court House. The Confederate commander arrived there first, and Grant left the choice of meeting place to him. Waiting under an apple tree on the edge of the village, Lee sent his aide, Lt. Col. Charles Marshall, to look for a suitable location, and Marshall settled on the large brick house of Wilmer McLean. Oddly enough, McLean had moved to Appomattox in 1863 to escape the conflict. His former home stood along Bull Run near Manassas, which also happened to be the site of two major battles.

Lee arrived at the McLean house around 1300. Clad in his full dress uniform, he was accompanied only by Colonel Marshall. Grant—his headache now gone, apparently cured by Lee's earlier message seeking surrender terms—arrived at McLean's home a half hour later along with several of his staff and general officers, including Ord, Sheridan, and Capt. Robert T. Lincoln, the president's eldest son. The Union commander did not have time to retrieve his dress uniform, so he appeared without a sword and wearing his field uniform, spattered with mud.

After some small talk about their service in the Mexican War, the two generals began to discuss the details of Lee's surrender. Grant proposed lenient terms for Lee's soldiers, who would be paroled and sent to their homes, "not to be disturbed by United States authorities so long as they observe their paroles." He allowed officers to keep their side arms, horses, and personal property. Upon Lee's request, Grant also permitted Confederate enlisted men to keep their personally owned mules and horses, which they would need for planting a crop that spring. The Union commander also promised to supply Lee's famished army with 25,000 rations, the bulk of which came from Confederate supplies captured at Appomattox Station. Grant put these terms into writing and both commanders agreed to designate subordinates to supervise the surrender and parole procedures. The meeting ended at 1500. Lee rode solemnly back to his headquarters in the woods near Longstreet's camp north of the Appomattox River, while Grant paused to telegraph the momentous news to Secretary of War Edwin M. Stanton. The Union commander left for City Point and Washington the next day, after an hour-long conversation with Lee between the opposing lines.

McLean House, Appomattox Court House, Virginia
(Library of Congress)

Upon hearing of Lee's capitulation, most of the Federal troops erupted in celebration. "Men shouted until they could shout no longer," a New York officer recalled, and Union artillery batteries fired thunderous salvos in honor of the occasion. General Meade himself rode along the lines shouting, "It's all over, boys! Lee's surrendered!" Out of respect for the defeated enemy troops, however, Grant

65

quickly banned these joyous demonstrations as inappropriate. The general in chief told his staff that "the best sign of rejoicing after the victory will be to abstain from all demonstrations in the field."

Within the rebel camps, men reacted to the war's end with a mixture of relief, sadness, and disbelief. "My disappointment was great," wrote a Southern cannoneer. "All this sacrifice of life—all this suffering had been for nothing, I thought. I sat down and wept." The next day, Lee issued a final order to his army, "General Order No. 9," praising his troops for "four years of arduous service, marked by unsurpassed courage and fortitude." The general "did not see how a surrender could have been avoided," he informed President Davis three days after the capitulation, given the lack of "subsistence for man or horse," and a dwindling army filled with "worn and exhausted" soldiers.

Grant ordered Union forces to move to Burkeville, retaining only a cavalry contingent and the V and XXIV Corps at Appomattox Court House to oversee the enemy's surrender. On the morning of 12 April, just over 28,000 officers and men of the Army of Northern Virginia, led by General Gordon's Second Corps, stacked arms and colors in a field near the courthouse, and then headed home with parole slips granting them safe passage. Although some 175,000 Confederate troops remained in the field, Grant rightly perceived that Lee's surrender marked the end of the bloody four-year struggle between the North and the South. "The war is over," he told his staff officers shortly after leaving the McLean house on 9 April, and "the Rebels are our countrymen again."

Analysis

The Union Army's ten-month struggle to capture Petersburg, the Confederacy's key supply hub in the Eastern Theater, ended in victory following General Lee's decision to abandon that city and Richmond in early April 1865. Although commonly referred to as a siege, General Grant's campaign to take the rebel capital and logistical center was more a series of operations intended to force Lee to abandon his defenses and fight a culminating battle in the open. A traditional siege involves surrounding a foe's defenses and cutting off his access to supplies and reinforcements. The Confederates at Richmond and Petersburg were neither surrounded nor cut off from their supplies, and Federal operations sought to pry the defenders out of their earthworks rather than contain them there.

Much was made by Southern partisans after the war—and by historians since—about the disparity in numbers between the two armies from the opening of the Petersburg Campaign in June 1864 to Lee's surrender in April 1865. In his farewell message to his troops, Lee wrote that his army was "compelled to yield to [the] overwhelming numbers and resources" of the Federals. After the war, Lee's former adjutant, Col. Walter Taylor, stated that Grant's forces were more than double the size of Lee's. In truth, the two belligerents were more closely matched. In early 1865, Lee had a peak strength of roughly 75,000 men under his immediate command, whereas the opposing Federal forces numbered about 120,000 soldiers. During the pursuit to Appomattox, Lee's army had to face only 80,000 bluecoats.

Although superior Union numbers was one factor in Lee's defeat, Federal success also stemmed from Grant's persistent operations against Lee's flanks, a powerful mounted force under General Sheridan that overtook Lee after the fall of Petersburg, and an inadequate Confederate logistical system. With a few conspicuous exceptions, Grant eschewed massed frontal assaults against the Southerners' imposing Petersburg defenses. Rather, he attacked the enemy's supply lines with cavalry raids and infantry expeditions, while repeatedly feinting on Richmond to draw off troops from Petersburg, his actual objective. Although slow and costly at times, the Federals' gradual extension of their lines to the west ultimately led to the capture of Lee's critical supply routes. Union operations also thinned the enemy's defenses to the point that the final Federal attacks at Five Forks on 1 April and on Lee's right at Petersburg the next day quickly overwhelmed the insufficient Confederate forces there.

Lee's evacuation of his fortifications on 2 April and his subsequent effort to reach both Johnston's army and several waiting supply stores was an attempt to concentrate Southern forces in a desperate bid to defeat the combined armies of Grant and Sherman. Grant's final campaign succeeded because Sheridan's hard-driving cavalry was able to intercept Lee's retreating column at Appomattox while Meade's infantry maintained its relentless pursuit from the rear. As a result, Lee had no choice but to yield on 9 April and obtain the best terms he could from Grant, a general known for demanding the "unconditional surrender" of his beaten enemies.

Despite Grant's uncompromising reputation and intense pressure from the radical Republican faction in Congress to punish the South for the crime of rebellion, the Union commander offered lenient terms to the defeated enemy soldiers camped around Appomattox Court House. Apparently most of the rebels were surprised by Grant's magnanimity. Lee felt that the terms would "do much toward conciliating our people," while a Confederate artilleryman called them "generous, considerate, and unlooked for." Recognizing that the war was all but over, Grant—with Lincoln's approval—acted on principals of reconciliation rather than retribution, and thus eased the difficult path for the North and the South to reunite after the guns fell silent.

THE AUTHOR

John R. Maass is a historian at the U.S. Army Center of Military History. He received a B.A. in history from Washington and Lee University, an M.A. in history from the University of North Carolina-Greensboro, and a Ph.D. in early American history from the Ohio State University. He is the author of *The French and Indian War in North Carolina: The Spreading Flames of War*, and *Defending a New Nation, 1783-1811*.

FURTHER READINGS

Calkins, Chris M. *The Appomattox Campaign: March 29–April 9, 1865.* Conshohocken, Pa.: Combined Books, 1997.

Grant, Ulysses S. *Personal Memoirs of U. S. Grant.* 2 Vol. New York: Charles L.Webster and Company, 1885.

Greene, A. Wilson. *Breaking the Backbone of the Rebellion: The Final Battles of the Petersburg Campaign.* Mason City, Iowa: Savas Publishing, 2000.

Marvel, William. *Lee's Last Retreat: The Flight to Appomattox.* Chapel Hill: University of North Carolina Press, 2002.

Slotkin, Richard. *No Quarter: The Battle of the Crater, 1864.* New York: Random House, 2009.

Trudeau, Noah Andre. *The Last Citadel: Petersburg, Virginia, June 1864–April 1865.* Boston: Little, Brown, 1991.

For more information on the U.S. Army in the Civil War, please read other titles in the U.S. Army Campaigns of the Civil War series published by the U.S. Army Center of Military History (www.history.army.mil).

Made in the USA
Monee, IL
09 December 2019